CULTURES OF THE WORLD
Colombia

mc **Marshall Cavendish**
Benchmark
New York

PICTURE CREDITS
Cover: © Jeremy Horner / CORBIS
Carlos Adampol Galindo / Flickr: 95 • Corbis / Click Photos: 17, 27, 29, 42 • Getty Images: 31, 33, 71, 73, 86, 96, 99, 120, 128 • Inmagine: 5, 7, 26, 38, 40, 45, 53, 55, 58, 68, 69, 74, 77, 81, 83, 92,100, 102, 103, 104, 105, 106, 107, 111, 112, 114, 115, 122, 123, 124, 126 • Marshall Cavendish International (Asia): 89, 108 • Photolibrary: 1, 3, 9, 10, 11, 12, 13, 14, 15, 16, 18, 19, 20, 22, 25, 30, 36, 37, 41, 43, 48, 51, 60, 61, 62, 63, 65, 66, 67, 70, 75, 76, 79, 80, 82, 84, 85, 87, 93, 98, 110, 118, 119, 121, 125, 129, 130, 131 • Topfoto: 24

PRECEDING PAGE
Towering mountain peaks surround this large lagoon in the Laguna Grande de la Sierra in the Sierra Nevada del Cocuy, Colombia.

Publisher (U.S.): Michelle Bisson
Writers: Jill DuBois, Leslie Jermyn, Yong Jui Lin
Editors: Deborah Grahame-Smith, Mindy Pang
Copyreader: Tara Tomczyk
Designers: Nancy Sabato, Benson Tan
Cover picture researcher: Tracey Engel
Picture researcher: Joshua Ang

Marshall Cavendish Benchmark
99 White Plains Road
Tarrytown, NY 10591
Website: www.marshallcavendish.us

© Times Media Private Limited 1990. First Edition.
© Times Media Private Limited 2002. Second Edition.
© Marshall Cavendish International (Asia) Private Limited 2012. Third Edition.
® "Cultures of the World" is a registered trademark of Times Publishing Limited.

Originated and designed by Times Media Private Limited
An imprint of Marshall Cavendish International (Asia) Private Limited
A member of Times Publishing Limited

Marshall Cavendish is a trademark of Times Publishing Limited.

Library of Congress Cataloging-in-Publication Data
DuBois, Jill, 1952-
    Colombia / Jill DuBois, Leslie Jermyn, and Yong Jui Lin. — 3rd ed.
       p. cm. — (Cultures of the world)
    Includes bibliographical references and index.
    Summary: "Provides comprehensive information on the geography, history,
       wildlife, governmental structure, economy, cultural diversity, peoples,
       religion, and culture of Colombia"—Provided by publisher.
    Includes bibliographical references and index.
    ISBN 978-1-60870-801-7 (print) -- ISBN 978-1-60870-808-6 (ebook)
    1. Colombia--Juvenile literature. I. Jermyn, Leslie. II. Yong, Jui Lin. III. Title. IV. Series.

F2258.5.D83 2012
986.1— dc23   2011023037

Printed in Malaysia
7 6 5 4 3 2 1

CONTENTS

COLOMBIA TODAY

WITH A POPULATION OF MORE THAN 45 MILLION PEOPLE, Colombia has the 30th-largest population in the world and the second-largest population in South America, after Brazil. Colombia is a land of contrasts and contradictions: its breathtaking beauty versus its miserable slums, its elaborate shows of courtesy and its uncontrolled violence, its torrid jungles and ice-covered peaks, its widespread poverty (although not the worst in Latin America) and the considerable happiness of its people. It has a strong tradition of democracy but it is dependent upon a ruling oligarchy to produce its leaders. It has produced phenomenal artists and infamous criminals. It is an unusually difficult nation to govern, with relatively weak institutions (a weak and poorly paid army, corrupt courts, an "informal" economy that overshadows the official economy, paramilitaries, guerrillas, drug traffickers, and so on), and it suffers from *centralización*, the need for everything to pass through the capital and largest city, Bogotá, before it is redistributed around the rest of the country.

Colombia has the third-largest population of the Spanish-speaking countries in the world, after Mexico and Spain. Colombia is the only country in South America with coastlines on both the North Pacific Ocean and the Caribbean Sea. Colombia is a standing middle power with the fourth-largest economy in Latin America. However, inequality and unequal distribution of wealth are still widespread.

Colombia is extremely ethnically diverse, and the interaction between descendants of the original native inhabitants, Spanish colonists, Africans who were brought as slaves, and 20th-century immigrants from Europe and the Middle East has produced a rich cultural heritage. This has also been influenced by Colombia's varied geography. The majority of the urban centers are located in the highlands of the Andes Mountains, but Colombian territory also encompasses Amazon rain forest, tropical grassland, and both Caribbean and Pacific coastlines. Ecologically, Colombia is one of the world's 17 mega-diverse countries (the most biodiverse per unit area).

Colombia is bordered to the east by Venezuela and Brazil, to the south by Ecuador and Peru, to the north by Panama and the Caribbean Sea, and to the west by Ecuador and the Pacific Ocean.

Part of the Ring of Fire, a region of the world subject to earthquakes and volcanic eruptions, Colombia is dominated by the Andes Mountains. Beyond the Colombian Massif (in the southwestern departments of Cauca and Nariño) the Andes are divided into three branches known as cordilleras (mountain ranges): the Cordillera Occidental, running adjacent to the Pacific coast, including the city of Cali; the Cordillera Central, running between the Cauca and Magdalena river valleys (to the west and east, respectively), including the cities of Medellín, Manizales, Pereira, and Armenia; and the Cordillera Oriental, extending northeast to the Guajira Peninsula, including the cities of Bogotá, Bucaramanga, and Cúcuta. At 8,612 feet (2,625 meters), Bogotá is the highest city of its size in the world.

In the east of the Andes lies the savannah of the llanos, part of the Orinoco River basin, and in the far southeast lies the jungle of the Amazon rain forest. Together these lowlands comprise more than half of the Colombia's territory, but they contain less than 3 percent of the population. To the north, the Caribbean coast, home to 20 percent of the population and the location of the major port cities of Barranquilla and Cartagena, generally consists of low-lying savannah, but it also contains the Sierra Nevada de Santa Marta mountain range, which includes the country's tallest peaks (Pico Cristóbal Colón and Pico Simón Bolívar), and the Guajira Desert. In contrast the narrow and discontinuous Pacific coastal lowlands, backed by the Serranía de Baudó Mountains, are covered with dense vegetation and are sparsely populated. The principal Pacific port is Buenaventura.

It is important to note that Colombia is a country of civil conflict. Although the situation has improved in the years following 2002, there are still many areas of the country that are considered too dangerous for tourism. Heavy day-to-day fighting between guerrillas, narco-traffickers (drug traffickers), paramilitaries, and state forces takes place in most of southern, southeastern, and northwestern Colombia as of 2010, including certain small urban centers such as those in the Choco department. Rural areas bordering Venezuela are also to be avoided. It is not considered safe to travel by bus across the country; instead domestic airlines such as Avianca are to be preferred. Some of the cities of Colombia are as follows:

The *palenqueras* in Colombia bring together elements of Spanish and African culture through their colorful clothing.

- **BOGOTÁ** Bogotá is the third-highest capital city in the world at 8,612 feet (2,625 m) above sea level and has an average temperature of 57.2°F (14°C). Bogotá hosts various internationally acclaimed events such as the Iberoamerican Theater Festival and the Rock al Parque, a concert featuring rock stars from around the globe. The city also offers a great variety of restaurants and museums, such as the Andrés Carne de Res.
- **BARRANQUILLA** This is Colombia's Golden Port and capital of the Atlántico department. Barranquilla holds its world famous Carnival each February.
- **CALI** Cali is Colombia's third-largest city and a center for the sugar and coffee industries. It enjoys terrific nightlife in the salsa clubs, and it proclaims itself to be the salsa capital of Latin America.

- **CARTAGENA** The old city walls and fortifications of Cartagena are the most extensive tourist destinations in South America. The old city is divided into three zones. San Pedro has the Cathedral de San Pedro Claver and many Andalusian-style palaces. San Diego is the old commercial precinct, where merchants, traders, and the middle class lived. Gethsemani is the living quarters of the working class. Cartagena was inscribed as a UNESCO World Heritage Site during the Eighth Session of the World Heritage Committee in Buenos Aires, Argentina, from October 29 to November 2, 1984.
- **LETICIA** Leticia is the capital of the Amazonas department. This is the place to experience the Colombian Amazon in its fullest glory.
- **MEDELLÍN** Medellín is the City of Eternal Spring and the capital of the Antioquia department. It is famous for having a large textile industry, which produces top-quality clothing that is sent all over the world. The birthplace of master painter Fernando Botero, it houses the great majority of his works.
- **PEREIRA** This is the capital of the Risaralda department and a major city of the coffee region. It is home to the Matecana Zoo. It is the jumping-off point for the Santa Rosa hot water springs and the Los Nevados National Natural Park.
- **POPAYÁN** This beautiful, whitewashed city is Colombia's religious center. It is home to the second-largest Easter festival in the world (after Seville in Spain). This town holds the record for producing the most Colombian presidents. It is bordered by the Puracé National Park and is a gateway to the archaeological sites of San Agustín and Tierra Dentro in nearby Huila.
- **SANTA MARTA** This is one of the major tourist centers of Colombia. It is unique in the sense that you could be walking on a beautiful beach one day, and the next day you could be at the foothill of a snowy mountain, the Sierra Nevada de Santa Marta, the highest in the country. It is also the place where General Simón Bolívar died, at La Quinta de San Pedro Alejandrino.

The most extensive influence on Colombian cuisine is Spanish. There are also influences from Peru, Brazil, Japan, and the Middle East. To this the Colombians add their own Amerindian cultural heritage.

Colombian food varies from region to region, but in general it relies on natural flavors and is not too spicy. Colombians also love soups, which are practically a must at dinner or lunch. But the most important fact is that Colombians love their food prepared with fresh ingredients and fruit.

In Bogotá and the Andean region, *ajiaco* is a traditional dish. It is a soup made of chicken, corn, and many different types of potatoes, avocado, and *guascas*, a local herb. Traditionally cream and capers are added before eating. *Ajiaco* is served with white rice, salad with a hint of lemon, avocado, or sweet or salty tostadas. For breakfast, people in Bogotá often eat *changua*, a milk, scallion, and egg soup. *Arepas*, South American corn cakes, and *pandebonos*, Colombian cheese bread, are also very popular.

The city of Medellín lights up at dusk. Medellín has overcome the handicaps of physical isolation and rugged terrain to develop into a flourishing city.

Along the Caribbean coast pork and whale liver are used in mild spicy food. Coconut rice is a common dish along the coastal cities. *Suero*, which is a blend of yogurt and sour cream, was introduced by Arab immigrants in Barranquilla and other coastal cities and is widely consumed. In the llanos of the east, barbecued meat is common due to the cowboy-like culture. Freshwater fish such as the amarillo are also eaten.

In the Amazon, Brazilian and Peruvian influences can be seen in the local food. Local resources such as beef and other livestock, as well as freshwater fish, are typical ingredients in Amazonian cuisine.

Tolimenses are considered a delicacy in the Tolima region. These tamales are made of corn dough and are filled with a mixture of peas, carrots, potatoes, rice, chicken, pork, and various spices. They are wrapped in plantain leaves and boiled for 3 to 4 hours. *Lechona* is a whole roasted pig stuffed with rice, peas, potatoes, and spices and is typically eaten on Sundays. This dish is now enjoyed throughout the country.

GEOGRAPHY

A panoramic view of Pasto Valley at the Andes. Pastos is the point where the Andes mountain range splits into the three cordilleras running down the length of Colombia.

COLOMBIA IS THE ONLY COUNTRY in Latin America named after Christopher Columbus, the European explorer who "discovered" the Americas. Located in the northwestern part of the South American continent, the country has Panama to the north, Venezuela and Brazil to the east, and Peru and Ecuador to the south as neighbors.

1

Colombia is the only South American country that borders both the Atlantic and Pacific oceans.

The Tairona National Park is an untouched area of jungle at the foot of the Sierra Nevada de Santa Marta, a mountain that drops abruptly into the Caribbean Sea.

With a total surface area of 439,736 square miles (1,138,910 square kilometers), approximately the combined area of Texas, Oklahoma, and New Mexico, Colombia is the fourth-largest country in South America. Colombian territory includes eight islands: Gorgona, Gorgonilla, and Malpelo in the Pacific Ocean; and San Andrés, Providencia, San Bernardo, Islas del Rosario, and Isla Fuerte in the Caribbean Sea.

TOPOGRAPHY

The distinguishing feature of Colombia is the Andes mountain chain in the central and western regions. Cordilleras, or mountain ranges, divide the country down its length. Cordillera Oriental (Eastern Range) is the longest range and the massive Cordillera Central is the highest range. The Cordillera Occidental (Western Range) is close to the frontier with Ecuador. Snow covers the summits of the central and eastern ranges, which also have volcanoes. The country is also divided by river systems. The river basins between the mountain ranges contain Colombia's three most important rivers: the Atrato, Cauca, and Magdalena. The Magdalena is historically known as the lifeline of Colombia. The river rises in the Andes, flows northeast about 960 miles (1,538 km) between the central and eastern ranges, and empties into the Caribbean. Although it is full of falls, sandbars, eddies, and sunken rocks, it is channeled so that large vessels can travel as far as Honda on the northern Caribbean coastline. The Cauca is the second most important river, with a valley that feeds most of the country. The other two great rivers are the Amazon and the Orinoco.

In the late 1980s approximately 78 percent of the country's population lived in the Andean highlands.

CLIMATE

About half of Colombia's land surface is characterized by mountains, high plateaus, and cool valleys. Because the country is situated close to the equator, the climate of its various regions is determined mainly by altitude. The coastal and eastern plains, known as los llanos, are at low altitudes and enjoy a tropical climate. The northernmost area of the Andes mountain chain experiences annual temperatures of 65°F (18°C) to 70°F (21°C). This temperate region is largely devoted to agriculture. Small coffee plantations lie on the craggy hillsides, and houses stand in the less tillable areas.

The cold regions, situated between 6,000 and 9,000 feet (1,829 and 2,743 m) above sea level, experience an average temperature of 53°F (11.7°C). Above 9,000 feet (2,743 m) temperatures fall below 50°F (10°C) and the land at this height is too cold for farming and can only be used for grazing. The snow line begins at about 15,000 feet (4,572 m).

The two coasts of Colombia vary greatly in the amount of rainfall each receives. La Guajira, at the northern tip of the country, is the driest place in Colombia, with an average annual rainfall of only 10 inches (25.4 centimeters). On the other hand cities in Chocó receive an average annual rainfall of nearly 400 inches (1,016 cm).

In the 1980s only 3 percent of all Colombians resided in the Pacific lowlands, a region of jungle and swamp with considerable but little-exploited potential in minerals and other resources.

This land of contrasts features deserts, windswept plains, wet rain forests, and snowcapped mountains.

FAUNA

Tapirs, ocelots, armadillos, and many other exotic animals thrive in the tropical areas of Colombia. Several types of monkey are also found in the rain forests. Some, however, such as the brown-headed spider monkey and Brumback's night monkey, are now threatened species.

Macaws, jacamars, cotingas, toucans, and many other birds with bright and colorful plumage make their nests in Colombia. The country has more than 1,500 species of bird—more than anywhere else in the world. Colombia is home to 18 percent of the world's bird species. These range from the tiny hummingbird, the gorgeted puffleg, only 3.5 inches (90 millimeters) long, to the large harpy eagle, which eats sloths, monkeys, opossums, and guinea pigs. The graceful Andean condor can also be seen soaring over the mountains of Colombia.

The rivers and their tributaries contain fish and mammals, such as stingrays and dolphins that are usually found in the open sea. The freshwater

Egrets and great blue herons flock around the Magdalena River.

fish vary greatly in size, from the tiny guppy and neon tetra to the arapaima, also known as pirarucu, the largest freshwater fish in the world. Colombia's waters are also home to large schools of flesh-eating piranhas.

FLORA

So much variety in climate enables diverse flora to flourish in Colombia. More than 130,000 species of plants have been found within Colombian territory. This includes around 3,000 types of orchids that are grown in the country. Cacti grow in the northern deserts, some reaching 60 feet (18 m) in height. In the central plains are vast woodlands. On the Caribbean coast are mangroves and coconut palms.

The toucan, with its characteristic bill, is one of the many kinds of bird found in Colombia.

Orchids with large, vividly colored flowers form a lush undergrowth in the dense Amazonian forest. This tropical region yields ipecac, quinine, and castor beans, used for medicinal purposes, and fruit such as papaya, mango, melon, pineapple, passion fruit, and banana. Rubber, chicle, vanilla, ginger, and sarsaparilla also come from this region. Other kinds of plants, virtually unknown in the United States, such as *curuba* (coo-ROO-bah), *chirimoya* (che-re-MOH-yah), *guanabana* (goo-ah-NAH-ba-nah), *zapote* (sah-POH-tay), and *granadilla* (grah-nah-DEEL-lyah), are also cultivated in Colombia.

The country's temperate regions produce flowers such as roses, chrysanthemums, and hortensia, which bloom throughout the year. Coffee plantations are located on the mountain slopes, and various small trees are planted to shade the coffee bushes. Eucalyptus, originally imported from Australia, grows well in the temperate regions. The windy, cold *páramos* (PAH-rah-mos), or high plains, of the *tierra fría* (tee-ERR-rah FREE-ah) are covered with low vegetation of vine shrubs, mosses, and resinous woody plants.

Nomads working a salt flat at Manaure in the Guajira Peninsula.

MINERAL WEALTH

Mineral deposits abound in Colombia. The country is the world's major source of emeralds and ranks fifth in the world in platinum production and ninth in gold. Other significant reserves include petroleum, silver, copper, lead, iron, mercury, nickel, and uranium.

Colombia is also beginning to benefit from one of its most undeveloped regions, the Guajira Peninsula, located on the northeastern corner of Colombia's Caribbean coast. Poor agricultural conditions have prevented the area from being cultivated, although an active salt mine has been there for years. Recently, however, geologists have discovered that the peninsula is rich in mineral deposits. Unexploited stores of natural gas, coal, and limestone have turned a desert into an economic oasis. The fields of the Guajira Peninsula are currently producing more than 80 percent of the natural gas used in the country's northern coastal region.

Blessed with mountains and rivers, Colombia has become one of the largest producers of hydroelectricity in Latin America. An ambitious program to develop hydropower is under way. However, supply has still fallen short of demand.

It was a quiet night in the central Colombian town of Armero, and most of the 22,000 residents were asleep when the downpour began. But it was not rain that was falling; it was volcanic ash pouring over the whole town. This unusual occurrence in November 1985 marked the beginning of the eruption of Nevado del Ruiz, a volcano in the Cordillera Central that had remained dormant for more than a century. Nobody could have imagined that over the next few frightening hours, Armero would transform from being a home to being a grave for nearly all its citizens.

The roar of destruction echoed through the town, and a torrent of molten mud and rock filled the streets. The eruption of the Arenas crater inside the 18,000-foot (5,486-m) peak melted the mountain's icecap, sending devastating mudslides and floods rushing down into the Chinchina and Lagunilla river valleys.

The eruption of Nevado del Ruiz killed 22,800 people and destroyed 50,000 acres (20,234 hectares) of farmland, 20,000 head of cattle, and 5,000 buildings. The town of Armero was virtually buried under mud, and several smaller towns in the area were nearly destroyed.

The enormity of the devastation made the grim task of searching for survivors practically impossible. Those who had fled to the hillsides to await evacuation by helicopter were clad in underwear or nightclothes encrusted with mud and covered with blood.

What made the disaster even more pitiable was that five weeks before the eruption, American and Italian volcanologists had warned Colombian authorities that Nevado del Ruiz, dormant since 1845, might come to life soon. Minor eruptions had occurred two months before the catastrophe, and government officials had begun evacuation plans and the plotting of likely paths of mudslides.

But the mountain did not wait.

CITIES

Colombia's largest cities are Bogotá, with a population of 8.5 million; Medellín and Cali, with a population of 3.3 million and 2.7 million, respectively; and Barranquilla, with a population of 1.9 million. Other large cities include Cartagena, Bucaramanga, Cúcuta, Manizales, Pereira, Santa Marta, and Ibagué. Many Colombian cities have grown rapidly in recent years. Immigration from rural areas has raised the country's urban population to 80 percent of the total population. The number of large cities in Colombia is uncharacteristic of Latin America. In most Latin American countries the capital and two or three other cities usually account for most of the urbanization.

BOGOTÁ

The full name of Colombia's capital is Santa Fe de Bogotá. The name *Bogotá* derives from the original Indian name, *Bacatá*, meaning "beyond the cultivated lands." Like many other cities Bogotá is a sprawling metropolis. It is situated in a high valley called the *Sabana de Bogotá*, at an altitude of more than 8,500 feet (2,591 m) above sea level.

The central district of the city of Bogotá Nuevo. Colombia's capital city is the focal point of all political, economic, and cultural activity in the country.

Bogotá is the artistic, cultural, intellectual, and political center of Colombia. It is also becoming a major industrial center. As one of the oldest cities in the Western Hemisphere, Bogotá is the site of many stately colonial churches, homes, and universities. Colombia's capital is divided into two cities—*Bogotá Viejo* (the old city) and *Bogotá Nuevo* (the new city). In the old quarter, scenic narrow streets lined with balconied buildings spread out from Plaza de Bolívar, the heart of Bogotá Viejo. This is where the first inhabitants lived.

Middle- and upper-class inhabitants live in ultra-modern buildings in the northern part of the city, where embassies, large private residences, and exclusive boutiques are also located. The broad boulevards, modern

skyscrapers, and shopping centers of Bogotá Nuevo create a stark contrast to the historical architecture of Bogotá Viejo. Working-class neighborhoods are in the southern and western areas of the city, where industrial plants are also located.

Bogotá has many museums tracing various aspects of Colombian art and history. The Colonial Museum has paintings of the Spanish colonial period. Handicrafts are exhibited at the Museum of Popular Arts and Traditions. Works done by the Indians of San Agustín are displayed at the National Museum. The Museo del Oro contains more than 25,000 gold objects, the world's largest collection of pre-Columbian goldsmiths' work.

As in other Colombian cities, streets in Bogotá run in straight lines and are called *calles* (KAHL-lyes) when running east to west and *carreras* (kar-REH-ras) when running north to south. The migration of people from the countryside has created *tugurios* (toor-GOO-ree-os), or slums. As in many other major cities, unemployment, poverty, and crime are common problems.

A view of Bogotá Viejo. Colombia's inhospitable terrain has resulted in high concentrations of people in the cities, where settlement is possible.

MEDELLÍN

Colombia's second-largest city is Medellín, known for its textile industry. In recent years it has become famous for being home to one of the largest

Cartagena, an old fortress city located on the Caribbean coast. The old and new harbors face each other.

cocaine-selling cartels. Just outside Medellín is El Ranchito, one of the world's outstanding collections of orchids.

Medellín was founded in 1616. Spaniards looking for opportunities to mine Medellín's gold deposits began settling there in the late 1600s. Many Colombians in Medellín today are descendants of these settlers. As the mines gave out, the early inhabitants quickly became proficient farmers. The region has become the leading coffee-growing area in the country.

Called the "City of Eternal Spring," Medellín has an agreeable climate and a dramatic mountain vista. There is a feeling of growth and prosperity about the city, which boasts many modern hotels, banks, offices, shops, and skyscrapers. Its flower-lined avenues are a pleasant surprise to visitors expecting to see the smokestacks of an industrial city. Medellín's bustling community is host to many flower festivals and exhibitions, and bullfights are a favorite pastime of the citizenry. On weekends during bullfighting season, La Macarena, a 10,000-seat bullring, is the center of much enthusiasm.

CALI

Founded in 1536, Cali is another of Colombia's old cities. This city has undergone exceptional growth over the last two decades, but many colonial buildings still stand. Cali is a manufacturing and distribution center that lies at the center of Cauca, the country's vital agricultural valley. The valley is responsible for 20 percent of Colombia's industrial output, consisting mainly of paper and sugar production. In spite of Cali's commercial focus, cultural and sporting endeavors are still popular.

At an altitude of 3,300 feet (1,006 m), Cali has a pleasant climate all year, with significant rainfall during its two rainy seasons. Flooding is a problem in lower sections of the city, and several earthquakes have hit Cali in the past few years. Some of Colombia's most hopeless slums are found in Cali. In the past dirt, disease, and poverty caused the death of half the city's children before they reached the age of five.

CARTAGENA

Cartagena is one of the most picturesque towns in South America and has some of the finest examples of 16th-century architecture in the Western Hemisphere. In its early days Cartagena was the most important fortified city of the Spanish Empire, and much of the fortification remains today. Sixteen miles (25.7 km) of protective wall surround narrow streets and adobe buildings, providing an exceptional view. On the one side is the Caribbean and on the other is the charming old section of the city. The contrast between old and new is prominent. Houses in the new part of Cartagena are of varied styles. Many are brightly colored two-story homes with attractive gardens, patios, and balconies. Within the old section remain seven fortresses that previously protected the harbor and the city. Street vendors and women carrying trays on their heads preserve the flavor of this picturesque place.

INTERNET LINKS

www.freeworldmaps.net/southamerica/colombia/map.html
This site contains a lovely map of Colombia with concise descriptions of the various regions.

http://geography.about.com/library/cia/blccolombia.htm
This site provides concise, precise information about the geography of Colombia.

www.123independenceday.com/colombia/geography.html
This site includes a first-rate summary of each of the regions of Colombia.

HISTORY

Mysterious ancient stone statues at San Agustín bear witness to Colombia's rich Indian heritage.

2

I N 1500 ALFONSO DE OJEDA BECAME the first European to reach the shores of what is now known as Colombia. At that time the area was inhabited by as many as eight different Indian groups, all of which spoke different languages.

• • • • • • • • •

Despite the country's commitment to democratic institutions, Colombia's history has been characterized by widespread, violent conflict.

The population at the time was possibly as large as 700,000. The most advanced of the people were the Chibcha, or Muisca, as they called themselves. They were mainly hunters and fishermen, but many lived by working the land and trading, and a good number were goldsmiths.

The coastal Indians proved so hostile that the earliest explorers withdrew quickly. But the exquisite gold ornaments fashioned by the Indians provided such a lure that Spanish explorers spread the word of a land of fabulous treasure—they called it *El Dorado*—hoping to bring the treasure back to Spain.

SPANISH SETTLEMENTS

The first permanent Spanish settlements were made at Santa Marta in 1525 and at Cartagena in 1533. However, the interior of the country was not penetrated until 1536, when Gonzalo Jiménez de Quesada traveled up the Magdalena River. He and his men defeated the Chibcha Indians they encountered in the various mountain valleys and founded the city of Bogotá in 1538.

At about the same time, an expedition from neighboring Ecuador, under the command of Sebastián de Benalcázar, had come up the Cauca Valley and founded Pasto, Popayán, and Cali. Another expedition led by Nicolaus de Federmann met up with Benalcázar's

THE LEGEND OF EL DORADO

The Chibcha, or Muisca, believe that a meteor hit the Earth and formed a great crater filled with water. In this lake, which is now called Guatavita, initiation rites were held for Chibcha chieftains. The chieftain's body was rubbed with a glue-like substance and was then covered with gold dust. The golden leader was then rowed to the middle of the lake aboard a raft holding gifts to the gods. On the shore, tribesmen knelt in awe among blazing bonfires. The new chief would then dive into the water and wash the gold dust into the lake as an offering to the deities. The treasures from the raft were added to the lake and the people on the shore added precious items of their own.

This simple Chibcha ceremony was the basis for the legend of El Dorado, *a term that now refers to any place where there is enormous wealth. The story inspired the Spanish to launch numerous explorations in search of these riches. The eventual conquest of the Chibcha ushered in Colombia as we know it today.*

group as they both reached Bogotá. This initiated a period of conflict among the various conquering groups.

Rather than fight, however, the three conquistadores, or conquerors, submitted their claims to the court of Spain. Federmann received nothing. Benalcázar was named governor of Popayán, and Jiménez de Quesada was given the military title of marshal and was allowed to remain on the land he had won for Spain. He named the newly conquered land *Nueva Granada* and its capital, Santa Fe de Bogotá.

The Castillo de San Felipe de Barajas in Cartagena. Cartagena was fortified to defend the country from attacks by English and Dutch pirates who coveted the gold being shipped to Spain.

NUEVA GRANADA

In 1550 a royal government was established for the administration of Colombia. In that same year gold was discovered in Antioquia. As soon as gold shipments to Spain commenced, English and Dutch pirates began to attack Spanish ships and Caribbean ports. However the interior of the country was able to develop undisturbed.

Despite Nueva Granada's great wealth, Spain was only mildly interested in this territory. For the first 200 years of Spanish rule, the land was governed by a president appointed by the viceroy of Peru.

During this time, however, Cartagena developed as the major port through which all trade with South America was supposed to travel. With the addition of the territory of present-day Ecuador and Venezuela, Colombia became a viceroyalty in its own right in 1739.

INDEPENDENCE

The movement for independence started in the 1790s, after the French Revolution. Venezuelans revolted in 1796 and 1806, but an attempt to set up an independent government in Bogotá failed.

Simón Bolívar, *El Libertador*, led the revolution that overthrew Spanish rule. His memory is held in great esteem throughout South America.

In May 1810 Cartagena declared independence. Bogotá followed suit on July 20, and six years of independence ensued. At that time Spain was involved in a war against France in Europe, but regained the territory in 1816. Finally Colombia got independence in August 1819 from Spain, when Simón Bolívar and his generals defeated the Spaniards at the Battle of Boyacá.

Bolívar and his generals, however, could not agree on a new form of government. Bolívar preferred a strong central government, whereas José Antonio Páez and Francisco de Paula Santander pushed for a federation of sovereign states. In 1821 the Constitution of Cúcuta formally set up the federation called the Republic of Colombia, which included Panama, Venezuela, and Ecuador. Within that Republic of Colombia, present-day Colombia was still known as Nueva Granada. It took the name of Colombia only in 1863. Historians refer to the former federation as Gran Colombia to avoid confusion.

Bolívar was the elected president of Gran Colombia, while continuing the fight for Ecuador's liberation and Peru's independence. In his absence Santander, his vice president, governed the nation.

DICTATORSHIP AND DEMOCRACY

The federation was doomed from the beginning. In 1827 Bolívar established a dictatorship but had to resign in March 1829 because of opposition. Two years later Santander became president and instituted a democratic state.

By 1849 two political parties were firmly established: the Conservatives, who were in favor of central government and closely tied with the Catholic Church, and the Liberals, who favored a federation of states and separation of church and state. From 1840 to 1880 the two parties alternated in power, amid much civil strife. But the economy and population prospered, and trade and communications gradually improved.

The poet Raphael Núñez was elected president in 1880. Although he was a declared Liberal, he held conservative views. Núñez ruled as a dictator until his death in 1894. He made Catholicism the state religion and restored a centralized government.

Meanwhile the local economy experienced little growth and in 1899 the War of a Thousand Days broke out. More than 100,000 people were killed, and the country was brought to the brink of economic collapse. Shortly after the restoration of peace, Panama seceded with the help of the United States. This interference resulted in bitter Colombian—American relations that lasted for many years.

Authorities surveying the dynamite- and fire-damaged Arauca village before the Colombian election in 1949. "La Violencia" from 1948 to 1958 is one of the bloodiest periods in Colombian history.

The period between 1903 and 1930 was unusually stable. Colombia developed a vigorous foreign trade, initially by exporting coffee. Multinational corporations invested in banana and petroleum production. Colombia experienced boom years in the 1920s. Railroads and power plants were built, but the affluence led to over-expansion and inflation.

LA VIOLENCIA

The Great Depression brought financial disaster. In 1930 the government began economic and social reforms. In 1944 a new labor code provided for minimum wages, employee benefits, and trade unions.

After World War II there were severe political crises, resulting in the assassination of popular leader Jorge Eliécer Gaitán in 1948. Thus began "La Violencia." It was a period of civil conflict in the Colombian countryside between supporters of the Colombian Liberal Party and the Colombian Conservative Party, a conflict that took place roughly from 1948 to 1958. In the next 10 years, some 200,000 persons lost their lives. A military coup in 1953 toppled the right-wing government of Conservative Laureano Gómez and brought General Gustavo Rojas Pinilla to power. Initially Rojas enjoyed considerable popular support, due largely to his success in reducing "La Violencia." When he did not restore democratic rule and occasionally engaged in open repression, he was overthrown by the military in 1957 with the backing of both political parties, and a provisional government was installed. An agreement called the *Frente Nacional* came into place. Under the accord, the Conservative and Liberal parties agreed to alternate the presidency for 16 years (four four-year presidential terms). Each four-year administration ruled over a coalition government. As this had its desired effect, it also sealed off political access to other smaller and more extreme parties, giving rise to the incessant guerrilla warfare of the past 50 years.

Left out of the Frente Nacional, smaller parties became disaffected and in the 1960s turned to a guerrilla conflict against the state. At the end of 1985 they united to form Unión Patriótica, which is now represented in the congress. The right-wing groups refused to accept these newly politicized guerrillas, and by the beginning of 1990, more than a thousand Unión Patriótica officials had been murdered. In June 1998 the Conservative opposition candidate, Andrés Pastrana Arango, son of former president Misael Pastrana Borrero, won the presidential vote in a runoff election. Pastrana Arango pledged to take a personal role in negotiations with rebel leaders, in an effort to end the civil conflict that raged for more than three decades and claimed at least 35,000 lives.

No single explanation fully addresses the deep roots of Colombia's present-day troubles, but some causes include limited government presence in large areas of the interior, the expansion of illicit drug cultivation, endemic violence, and social inequities. In May 2002 the former Liberal politician Álvaro Uribe, whose father had been killed by left-wing guerrillas, was sworn in as Colombian president. He immediately began taking action to crush the militant groups, including the employment of citizen informants to help the police and armed forces track down suspected members. The Revolutionary Armed Forces of Colombia (*Fuerzas Armadas Revolucionarias de Colombia*, FARC) is the leading left-wing revolutionary guerrilla organization based in Colombia. Its members have fought the government and caused instability in Colombia for many years.

In the fall of 2002 the administration released the much-awaited Colombian national security strategy, entitled the Democratic Security and Defense Policy. As of 2004, two years after its implementation began, the security situation in Colombia showed some measure of improvement and the economy, although still fragile, also showed some positive signs according to observers, but relatively little was yet accomplished in structurally solving most of the country's other grave problems. This is possibly in part due to legislative and political conflicts between the administration and the Colombian Congress (including conflicts over the controversial project to eventually re-elect Uribe), and a relative lack of freely allocated funds and credits. Uribe was re-elected in 2006 after a change in the constitution allowed re-election for presidents.

On May 30, 2010, the Colombian people voted for the former Minister of Defense Juan Manuel Santos to be the president from 2010 to 2014. He became Colombia's president on August 7, 2010, on a platform of reconciliation with guerrilla groups.

Trained as a lawyer, Álvaro Uribe Vélez was president of Colombia from 2002 to 2010.

INTERNET LINKS

http://colombiajournal.org/

This up-to-date *Colombia Journal* website provides balanced coverage on a wide range of articles on Colombia.

www.traveldocs.com/co/govern.htm

This site contains a concise and accurate summary of Colombia's history, government, and political condition.

www.factmonster.com/ipka/A0107419.html

This site includes an accurately detailed summary of Colombia's history, including U.S. and Venezuelan involvement.

GOVERNMENT

Colombia is a democratic country. The seat of the government is the Congress Building in Bogotá.

3

The Colombian Constitution of 1991 provides the framework for a welfare state and a unitary republic.

COLOMBIA IS A DEMOCRATIC republic with a centralized government and separate executive, legislative, and judicial branches. Its basic structure of national government is quite similar to that of the United States. It has a long history of democracy, which is quite notable in a continent known for dictatorships.

The president is elected by direct voting for a four-year term, and with the amendment introduced by Álvaro Uribe, can serve a maximum of two terms in succession. As the chief legislative executive, he has the power to approve or veto legislation. He appoints a cabinet of 13

Citizens casting their votes during the 2010 elections in Bogotá. Colombia's political scene is dominated by two parties, the Liberals and the Conservatives.

"In the name of God, supreme source of all authority, and for the purpose of strengthening national unity and securing the benefits of justice, liberty, and peace, we have decided to decree, and we do hereby decree, the following POLITICAL CONSTITUTION OF COLOMBIA."

Colombia has "control institutions" that mix government and public officials, who work alongside one another. For example, the public's Inspector General works closely with the government's Controller General, whose job is to ensure governmental fiscal responsibility.

ministers and is assisted in decision making by a 10-member consulting body called the Council of State. The president acts as commander in chief and directs internal affairs.

THE NATIONAL CONGRESS

The legislative branch is known as the National Congress—a bicameral (two-house) congress composed of the Chamber of Representatives and the Senate. Representatives and senators are elected to serve four-year terms. Each department, or state, is represented by two senators-at-large and an additional senator for every 200,000 people. There are two representatives for each department plus an additional one for every 100,000 people. Currently there are 102 senators and 161 representatives.

THE JUDICIARY

Until 1991 the basic law of Colombia was the constitution of 1886. This conservative document was supplanted by the more inclusive constitution of 1991. The system of courts includes a Supreme Court of Justice that tries cases involving interpretation of the constitution and impeachment. It also serves as the final court of appeal. Judges of this court are nominated by the president and elected by the congress. They are reappointed every five years.

Administratively Colombia is divided into 33 units, which includes 32 departments and the *Distrito Capital de Santa Fe de Bogotá*, or Capital District of Bogotá. Governors of each department are popularly elected and are included in the executive branch.

Juan Manuel Santos Calderón is the president of the Republic of Colombia. He was inaugurated on August 7, 2010, as the 40th president of Colombia.

In 1994 he founded the Good Government Foundation, whose stated objective was helping and improving the governability and efficiency of the Colombian government. This organization presented a proposal for a demilitarized zone and peace talks with the FARC guerrillas.

Santos also founded the Social National Unity Party (Party of the U) to support the presidency of Álvaro Uribe. He was named Minister of Defense on July 19, 2006. During his tenure, the administration dealt a series of blows against the FARC guerrilla group, including the rescue of Fernando Araújo Perdomo when he was kidnapped; the death of FARC leader Raúl Reyes on March 2, 2008; an air strike against a guerrilla camp located within Ecuador's borders; and the nonviolent rescue of former presidential candidate Ingrid Betancourt, who had been held captive since 2002, along with 14 other hostages.

At the local level mayors of cities are elected by popular voting. Deputies for assemblies of the various department and municipal councils are also chosen by direct voting.

VOTING AND ELECTIONS

Voting is open to all citizens above the age of 18 years. In August 1957 a special act was passed that allowed women to take part in national elections. Colombians must register their vote and have a citizenship card. Voting is considered a legal right but not a duty, and there are no literacy or land ownership requirements. In past elections participation has been as low as 30 percent. Members of the national police, active members of the armed forces, and a small number of people who have lost their political rights by law are not allowed to vote.

THE 2008 ANDEAN DIPLOMATIC CRISIS

The 2008 Andean diplomatic crisis was a diplomatic standoff between the South American countries of Ecuador, Colombia, and Venezuela. It began with an incursion by the Colombian military into Ecuadorian territory across the Putumayo River on March 1, 2008, leading to the deaths of more than 20 militants, including Raúl Reyes (one of the leaders of the FARC) and 16 other members of the FARC. This incursion led to increased tension between Colombia and Ecuador and the movement of Venezuelan and Ecuadorian troops to their borders with Colombia.

The military and diplomatic row ensued, ambassadors were recalled, and arrests were made worldwide following Colombians' seizure of laptop computers from the FARC camp that were found to contain a large number of letters and documents pertaining to FARC activities. Tensions increased in the region, and there was much hand-wringing and urging of peaceful reconciliation from neighboring countries. Happily the crisis ended at the Rio Group summit on March 7, 2008, with a public reconciliation among the three countries involved.

Voter registration takes place at the municipal level, which means that there are local offices to handle the process. Although the requirements for voting are not strict, registration is somewhat complicated, and re-registering after moving to another district is very tedious.

Polling places are supervised by a committee that consists of two members from each political party. Committees report the results to the municipal registrar, and the results are forwarded to the national registrar.

PLAN COLOMBIA

Plan Colombia refers to an aid initiative originally proposed by Colombian President Andrés Pastrana Arango. The plan included U.S. military/counter-narcotics aid, but was not just limited to that. Plan Colombia was conceived between 1998 and 1999 by the administration of Pastrana with the goals of ending the Colombian armed conflict and creating an anti-cocaine strategy.

Critics of the initiative claimed that elements within the Colombian security forces, which received aid and training from the United States, were involved in supporting or tolerating abuses by right-wing paramilitary forces against left-wing guerrilla organizations and their sympathizers. Another controversial element of the anti-narcotic strategy is aerial fumigation to eradicate coca (unrefined cocaine). This activity has come under fire because it damages legal crops and has adverse health effects upon those who are exposed to the herbicides.

In 2000 the Clinton administration in the United States supported the Plan Colombia initiative by committing $1.3 billion in foreign aid and up to 500 military personnel to train local forces. An additional 300 civilian personnel were allowed to assist in the eradication of coca. This aid was an addition to $330 million of previously approved U.S. aid to Colombia, and $818 million was earmarked for 2000, with $256 million for 2001. As of August 2004 the United States had spent $3 billion in Colombia, more than 75 percent of it on military aid. Before the Iraq War, Colombia was the third-largest recipient of U.S. aid after Egypt and Israel. The United States has 400 military personnel and 400 civilian contractors in Colombia.

INTERNET LINKS

http://ciponline.org/colombia/index.htm

This site gives up-to-date information on the Center for International Policy's efforts to assist Colombia with monetary aid and personnel.

www.state.gov/r/pa/ei/bgn/35754.htm

This U.S. Department of State site provides information about the government of Colombia, including a comprehensive section on international relations.

www.classbrain.com/art_cr/publish/colombia_government.shtml

This site includes concise information about how the government of Colombia works.

ECONOMY

A lowland coffee (*Coffea arabica*) plantation near Pereira in Colombia. Cultivation in the shade and picking by hand contribute to the high quality of Colombian coffee beans.

4

ECONOMIC DEVELOPMENT IN Colombia can be divided into four periods. The first ended in 1880, before which the country had no stable exports to help buy foreign goods.

Coffee paved the way for the second period, which lasted until 1930. Export of this plentiful commodity paid for manufactured goods from abroad. At this time industry also developed in Medellín.

The third period began during the Great Depression and was marked by industrialization on a national scale. Until 1967 the economic policy of the country stressed industrialization. Revenue from coffee was used to purchase intermediate goods, or materials for factories being developed.

In the present, fourth period, the government has encouraged the export of other goods to supplement coffee and refined petroleum, the country's main exports. Supplementary exports have become a

Container ship in the seaport of Buenaventura on Colombia's Pacific coast.

In spite of the difficulties caused by serious internal armed conflict, Colombia's market economy grew steadily in the latter part of the 20th century. The country suffered a recession in 1999 and the recovery from that recession was long and painful. However, in recent years, growth has been impressive, reaching 8.2 percent in 2007, one of the highest rates of growth in Latin America.

Another contribution to the Colombian economy is the export of fresh-cut flowers, which earns a substantial income.

reliable source of foreign currency. In 2011 the Colombian stock market declined by 8.8 percent. The official unemployment rate in 2010 reduced to 11.8 percent from 14.1 percent in 2009. President Santos has announced his intention to reduce the unemployment rate to 8 percent by offering tax breaks to employers.

THE MIXED ECONOMY

Private enterprise is stronger in Colombia than in most Latin American countries. In fact one of the most dynamic capitalist projects in Latin America took place around Medellín at the beginning of the 20th century. There was a surge in the growth of industrial plants, especially textile industries. The success of this venture convinced everyone that the government could not manage the economy alone and needed the aid of the private sector.

The government involves itself in the economy in unique ways. The Colombian economy is defined as a mixed economy. There are separate functions for the government, for private home-grown businesses, and for foreign multinational corporations. The government's role is considered essential to lead the nation to full development. The government owns transportation systems, roads, and telecommunications, and it produces and administers the country's electricity. As owner of the subsoil, the government is expected to develop energy resources. The government is also directly involved in the economy through its control of tariffs, taxation, and exchange rates.

An interesting aspect of the way the private sector operates in Colombia is that it does not invest in enterprises that are considered essential to national development. However, when these enterprises become profitable, the government sells them to private corporations.

AGRICULTURE

Colombia is primarily an agricultural nation, largely dependent on coffee. Thirty years ago about half of the population consisted of farmers. However, the peasants' terror of being killed or kidnapped by guerrilla, army, paramilitaries, or narcotraffickers has led to an emptying of the countryside and the unfortunate shift from Colombia's being a net exporter of produce to its being a net importer. Today 18 percent of the workforce is engaged in agriculture. One-quarter of the nation's land is used for agriculture, of which about 10 percent is devoted to crop production and the rest is utilized for livestock pasture. Colombia produces a wide range of crops, from bananas, which need warm temperatures, to potatoes, which flourish in a cooler climate. However, many people have to farm on inclines that erode easily, and deforestation in the Andean region is intensifying the erosion problem. Many farms in the highlands are quite small, and the owners rely on simple farming methods. Their traditional ways limit them to subsistence farming, which means that their work produces goods needed for the family, with no significant surplus for sale. Agriculture accounts for 9.3 percent of Colombia's GDP.

COFFEE Colombia is the world's third-largest producer of coffee. Colombian coffee is a protected designation of origin granted by the European Union (in September 2007) that applies to the coffee produced in Colombia. Colombian coffee has been recognized worldwide as having high quality and a distinctive taste. The main importers of Colombian coffee are the United States, Germany, France, Japan, and Italy. About one-sixth of all arable land in Colombia is dedicated to producing this crop, the second most profitable export after oil. Because coffee beans grow best between 4,300 and 6,600 feet (1,311 and 2,012 m), the greatest concentration of coffee farms is near Medellín. Coffee is a labor-intensive crop, and coffee farms are typically small.

Colombia is the second-largest producer of Arabica coffee in the world, after Brazil. With climate change, coffee yields have plummeted as a result of rising temperatures and more intense and unpredictable rains. Average temperature in Colombia's coffee regions has risen nearly 1°F (0.55°C) in 30

The National Federation of Coffee Growers of Colombia was formed in 1927. The joining of local farmers and small producers within the federation has permitted them to confront logistical and commercial difficulties that would not have been possible individually. The federation today generates income for more than 560,000 coffee-farming families.

Colombian workers preparing bananas for packaging on a banana plantation in Aracataca.

years, and in some mountain areas, the temperature increase has been doubled. At the new, higher temperature, the plants' buds abort or their fruit ripens too quickly for optimum quality. There is also coffee rust, a fungus that could not survive the cool mountain weather previously. The Coffee Growers Federation has advised farmers to switch to a newer, hardier strain of Arabica.

BANANAS Bananas, another significant export, are grown along the country's Caribbean coast. Among legal crops, this crop is believed to earn the farmer the best income return per acre. Foreign multinational corporations were initially involved in banana production. However, private Colombian organizations have also entered the market. As much as 40 percent of the total banana production is consumed domestically.

SUGARCANE Sugarcane, much of which is made into unrefined brown sugar, or *panela* (pah-NAY-lah), is planted throughout the warm areas of the nation, especially in the Cauca river valley and on the central Pacific coast.

In contrast to the well-defined growing season found in many other sugarcane regions in the world, Colombia's sugarcane harvest continues almost throughout the year. This is due to the constant hot and humid climate in the country's growing regions. Warm days and steady rainfall all year-round provide permanent employment for Colombian cane cutters.

FLOWERS

Fresh-cut flowers are another important commodity. This commercial activity is concentrated in the *sabana* (sah-BAH-nah), or treeless plain, near Bogotá. It provides employment for about 100,000 people. Colombian flower

A vaquero herds his cattle in the eastern llanos, one of the most important cattle-raising regions.

producers supply carnations, orchids, and other popular flowers for the export market. Colombia is the second-largest exporter of fresh-cut flowers in the world, after the Netherlands.

CATTLE

Livestock is mostly raised commercially in scattered areas throughout the country, although major concentrations are in the Sabana de Bogotá and the eastern plains.

Beef is the major meat produced in the country. In the early 1980s the cattle population was estimated to be more than 26 million, which means that there were almost as many cows as people.

Recently, however, cattle ranchers have faced a number of problems that have made it difficult for them to increase beef production. The high presence of illicit crops such as coca, marijuana, and poppies is a mammoth obstacle for the ranchers to overcome.

FISHING

Colombian fishermen catch mainly tuna, shrimp, and many freshwater species. The nation's annual fish catch, most of which comes from coastal fishing, is not as substantial as that of some other Latin American countries, such as Chile and Peru. Many observers believe that Colombia has much unrealized fishing potential. The country's fishing industry is active along the coasts and in the Magdalena river valley. Buenaventura and Tumaco are the main fishing ports.

Two-thirds of the cut flowers sold in the United States are imported from Colombia.

MINING

Colombia is well endowed with minerals. The country possesses significant amounts of nickel, gold, silver, platinum, and emeralds.

During the colonial period Colombia was a major contributor of gold to the Spanish coffers. Today Colombia accounts for about 80 percent of the world's emerald production.

Colombia is also a major South American producer of gold and has the world's largest platinum reserves. In addition to those already mentioned, today Colombia's wealth of minerals includes lead, mercury, manganese, coal, and salt.

The Guajira Peninsula has a valuable deposit of clean-burning coal. Because the coal is near the surface, it is easily mined by open-pit or strip-mining techniques. The Colombian government and several industrial firms have spent millions to develop this coal mine, which may store as much as 60 percent of South America's coal reserves.

ENERGY PRODUCTION

Oil wells in the Magdalena river valley have been supplying most of the nation's crude oil since the 1920s. Additional oil deposits have been discovered in numerous other areas, including the basin of the Catatumbo River, in the central Caribbean and Pacific areas, and in the eastern llanos.

These findings have led geologists to think that there may be more oil deposits near in the Andean region. In the mid-1970s Colombia began importing oil to augment its production. But the nation has now regained its self-sufficiency and has even become a modest exporter of oil since 1986.

To keep up with its energy demands, Colombia makes use of its waterways. The abundance of rivers, coupled with abundant rainfall, has led experts to say that Colombia has some of the greatest hydroelectric potentials in the world. Hydroelectric power facilities are located in the Bogotá-Cali-Medellín area, which is referred to as the "industrial triangle."

Miners at work at the Muzo emerald mine in Colombia. The subsoil of Colombia is extremely rich in minerals. It was mainly the abundance of gold that led to colonization by the Spanish.

Colombia has the largest coal reserves in Latin America.

As of 2004 Colombia had become a net energy exporter, exporting electricity to Ecuador and developing connections to Peru, Venezuela, and Panama as well.

The Cauca Valley Authority is headquartered in Cali. This corporation's focus is on flood control, improved farming techniques through irrigation, and the development of electrical power. This successful venture tripled Cali's electrical power in its first eight years. Currently about 75 percent of existing Colombian power systems use hydroelectric power, and there is potential to increase this to 90 percent.

TRANSPORTATION

Topography is a contributing factor to obstacles in transportation. The terrain of the Andes and landslides due to heavy rainfall in the heavily populated highlands make road and rail travel difficult and expensive to develop and maintain. In some areas mules are sometimes the only means of transporting people and goods across the terrain. In more developed spots, aerial cable cars are the main option. There are some other alternatives, however.

RIVER Travel by river is very important. In fact, before the railroad from Bogotá to Santa Marta was built, the Magdalena River was the major travel route between the Caribbean coast and the interior. Not too long ago almost 95 percent of all commercial inland water travel took place on

Colombia is the heart of the illegal drug trade in South America. The city of Medellín not only produces more cocaine than any other place in the world but is also the control center for most of the export operations to the United States.

The organization and production of cocaine have grown over the decades so that Colombia's drug barons have become extremely wealthy and powerful. At one stage they were known as the Medellín cartel, because it was believed that, as a group, they could fix the price of cocaine and control the markets. The Cali cartel ascended just as the Medellín cartel (headed by Pablo Escobar) fell. Rather than behave like gangsters, the Cali cartel bosses behave like businessmen, negotiating with corporations and even the government and influencing all of Colombian society. Since about 2005, much of the industry has been exported to northern Mexico, where it is easier to ship drugs into the United States. The demand for drugs in America is fuelling the drug trade in Colombia and around the world. However, there were huge amounts of money to be made and vast areas of land on which to cultivate the coca leaf so that many other growers and traffickers could also participate.

Colossal profits can be made from cocaine even without complete control. Cocaine is produced at $682 per pound ($1,500/kilogram) in jungle labs and could be sold on the streets of the United States for as much as $22,727 per pound ($50,000/kilogram). Within a year Colombian traffickers earn a total of between $7 billion and $16 billion from the pure cocaine they provide. In the United States this has a street value of more than 10 times than that amount. Almost all of the money is profit, because there is very little outlay in production. Something like $3 million worth in refining chemicals and coca leaves can make $1 billion in sold cocaine!

This fantastic wealth presents a tempting avenue out of poverty. Colombian peasants who grow coca leaves do not expect to make profits on the same scale as the drug barons make, but they can certainly expect to earn three to four times as much from their labor on coca plantations as they would from any other crop.

The Reagan and Bush administrations (1981—93) in the "war on drugs" campaign found it difficult to halt the expansion of the drug trade for the principal reason that many of the traffickers and workers were too poor to care about prison sentences. They had nothing to lose other than their poverty.

The drug barons used their money to gain influence and power in the Colombian government and army and among the people. By doing this, they protected themselves from legal problems. When the U.S. government wished to have the worst offenders extradited to the United States, immense support from Colombians for the "Extraditables" (paramilitary figures who face the U.S. government extradition requests for drug trafficking offences) prevented this.

The effects of cocaine production range from environmental damage to effects on education, health, and the country's economy. The environment is damaged through deforestation caused by clearing fields for cultivation. Soil erosion and chemical pollution also have effects on the Colombian economy. The issues are difficult to address because of the wealth and power of drug traffickers.

Despite the fact that Colombia has had the dubious distinction of being the world's leading producer of coca for many years, the various plans for the combined war on drugs have slowly but surely diminished the amount of drug produced to the extent that, in 2010, the country reduced cocaine production by 60 percent from 2000. Also in 2010 Peru surpassed Colombia as the main producer of coca leaves in the world. The level of drug-related violence was halved in the last 10 years, when the country moved from being the most violent country in the world to having a homicide rate that is lower than the rates in countries such as Honduras and Jamaica. The actions of the Colombian National Police against drug trafficking have been so effective that the country has captured and extradited drug lords at the rate of more than 100 per year for the last 10 years and currently gives technical advice to 7 countries in Latin America and 12 in Africa.

the Magdalena. In times of drought, however, this mode of transportation became impossible. The only means of transportation in 60 percent of the country is via waterways, but guerrilla groups control the waterways in the south and southeast.

ROAD The country has nearly 101,284 miles (163,000 km) of road, of which 68,885 miles (110,860 km) are paved. The irregular terrain makes the construction of roads a very costly venture. Despite serious terrain obstacles, almost three-quarters of all cross-border dry cargo is now transported by road.

There are, however, three important road systems that run north to south between the mountain systems. In addition the Simón Bolívar Highway, which is 2,300 miles (3,701 km) long, runs from Guayaquil in Ecuador, east through Colombia, to Caracas in Venezuela.

RAIL The National Railway System network, which is 2,363 miles (3,802 km) long, is almost completely owned by the government. Major extensive extensions to the railway in the 1940s and 1950s finally connected the highlands with both coasts. The Atlantic railway was opened in 1961 and runs from Bogotá to Santa Marta. Buenaventura and Bogotá are connected by the Pacific railway. Freight and passenger railway traffic reached its height in the 1960s, when truck and airline services surpassed rail traffic in popularity. The national railroad system, once the country's main mode of transport for freight, has been neglected in favor of road development and now accounts for only about a quarter of freight transport.

AVIATION To surmount the difficulties of cross-country travel due to the complex mountain systems, Colombia turned to air travel and became a trailblazer in the field of domestic civil aviation. In 1919 Colombia founded its own airline, Avianca, which is now the nation's major international airline. This thriving service flies directly to numerous cities in the United States, Canada, and Europe. Colombia has well-developed air routes and an estimated 984 airports, 100 of which have paved runways, plus two heliports. Bogotá's

El Dorado International Airport handles 386 short tons (350 million metric tons) of cargo and 8 million passengers a year, making it the largest airport in Latin America in terms of cargo and the third largest in passenger numbers.

FOREIGN TRADE

Colombia's imports are mainly raw materials and intermediate goods. Its major exports, as mentioned earlier, are coffee, coal, and fuel oil.

The United States and Colombia have long been major trading partners. Prior to 1950 more than 70 percent of Colombia's exports went to the United States, and more than 60 percent of its import activities involved goods from the United States. Currently 40 percent of Colombian exports go to the United States, and 45 percent of its imports come from the United States.

New markets have opened in Europe, and Colombia has played a key role in the Andean Common Market. This group's major goal is to reduce the trade restrictions among its member nations. Evidence of its success can be seen in the significant trading relationships between Colombia and its neighbors. As part of its economic strategy to diversify its export markets, Colombia is also in negotiations to sign a free trade agreement with China in late 2011.

INTERNET LINKS

www.classbrain.com/art_cr/publish/colombia_economy.shtml
This site contains a concise summary of Colombia's economy.

www.pbs.org/wgbh/pages/frontline/shows/drugs/business/inside/colombian.html
This site includes fascinating information on Colombia's drug cartels.

www.latinamericanstudies.org/colombia-drugs.htm
This site provides a number of archived articles and pictures on the drug trade in Colombia.

ENVIRONMENT

A river flowing through the Parque Natural El Gallineral in San Gil, Colombia.

5

COLOMBIA IS A LAND OF IMMENSE
environmental wealth and diversity.
It is also a country where issues of
the environment are closely tied to politics,
economics, and relations with the rest of
the world, especially the United States.

As the fourth-largest South American country, Colombia has an amazing diversity of plant and animal life. It ranks second after Brazil for having the greatest biodiversity—or variety of plant and animal species—in the world. Colombia is home to more than 1,500 bird species, representing nearly 20 percent of the world total, and around 50,000 plant species, including some 3,000 orchid species.

The reason for this incredible natural wealth is that Colombia has both Atlantic and Pacific coastlines, boasts highlands and lowlands, and experiences tropical, desert, and temperate climates. Its location means that Colombia is home to plants and animals from both South and Central America.

FASCINATING CREATURES

Colombia's varied ecosystems support a wide range of different animal species. Deserts in the north, grasslands in the east, swamps and wetlands in the northwest, dozens of river habitats throughout the country, and forests ranging from temperate to tropical, broad-leafed to coniferous, mountain to coastal, and mangroves to coconut palm groves—all form unique microenvironments, which host a diversity of plant and animal life, some of which are found nowhere else on Earth.

Along with Costa Rica, Colombia has been at the forefront of environmental management in Latin America. It was one of the first countries in the region to organize environmental administration along watershed boundaries, pilot a system of pollution taxes, require environmental impact assessments for large construction projects, and institutionalize legal remedies against polluters.

Colombia's animal life includes several species of monkey, wild cats, reptiles (such as the Orinoco and American crocodiles), bears, deer, tapirs, and armadillos. There are also hundreds of fresh and saltwater fish, including the fabled piranha and electric eel.

Some 1,550 species of birds have been recorded in Colombia—more than the total number of bird species found in the United States and Europe combined! Colombia's bird life ranges in size from the huge Andean condor that lives in the high mountains to tiny hummingbirds that inhabit the tropical forests.

CONSERVATION

Colombia has set aside approximately 8 percent of its territory for national parks, sanctuaries, and reserves. Examples are Los Flamencos, where pink flamingos stride in coastal lagoons, and Los Estoraques, with its rock formations. But much more needs to be done to protect indigenous flora and fauna.

Endangered species in Colombia include the tundra peregrine falcon, the Cauca guan, the gorgeted wood-quail, the red siskin, five species of turtle (green sea, hawksbill, olive ridley, leatherback, and arrau), two species of alligator (spectacled caiman and black caiman), and two species of crocodiles (American and Orinoco). By 2001, 35 of Colombia's 359 species of mammals, 64 of 1,770 breeding bird species, 15 reptile species out of 356, and 429 of 51,000 plant species were endangered.

EXTINCT ANIMALS

THE COLOMBIAN GREBE The Colombian grebe was an aquatic bird found in the Bogotá wetlands in the Eastern Andes of Colombia. The species was still abundant on Lake Tota (9,843 feet [3,000 m]) in 1945.

The decline of the Colombian grebe is attributed to wetland drainage, siltation, pesticide pollution, disruption by reed harvesting, hunting, competition, and predation of chicks by rainbow trout. The primary reason was loss of habitat: Drainage of wetlands and siltation resulted in

SYMBOL OF A NATION: THE ANDEAN CONDOR

The Andean condor is Colombia's national animal and the world's largest bird of prey; a fully grown adult weighs an average of 22 pounds (10 kg) and has a wingspan of at least 10 feet (3 m). It can fly 200 miles (322 km) a day at extremely high altitudes when searching for food.

Andean indigenous cultures revered this magnificent bird; in some cultures, killing a condor was a mark of manhood. The condor's habitat once included all of the Andes and the western coastline of South America. Now it is found only in parts of Peru, north and eastern Colombia, northern Venezuela, southern Patagonia (in the south of Colombia), Bolivia, and northern Ecuador. The bird has disappeared from much of its former range and is critically endangered where it is still found.

Andean condors are able to reproduce only when they reach 7 to 11 years of age. They then mate once every other year and build their nests at altitudes above 10,000 feet (3,000 m). In captivity, safe from human hunters, Andean condors can live as long as 70 years. They feed mainly on dead flesh, but sometimes they attack newborn animals and bird colonies as well. Because they have no voice box, condors cannot make normal bird calls, only wheezes and grunts.

Living in fragile high-altitude environments, the Andean condor leads a vulnerable existence. The expansion of human settlement destroys the bird's habitat. Also the condor sometimes attacks farm animals, and people hunt it as a pest, if not for its feathers. For the condor population to remain stable, each nesting pair must live long enough for their own offspring to start nesting. This means a lifespan of 25 to 30 years, which is becoming increasingly difficult for the birds to achieve, as people encroach upon their hunting and foraging grounds.

Sadly the
Colombian grebe
and the Caribbean
monk seal have
become extinct.

higher concentrations of pollutants in waterways. This destroyed the open pondweed vegetation and resulted in the formation of a dense monoculture of water weed.

By 1968 the species had declined to approximately 300 birds. Only two records of this bird were made in the 1970s; one was seen in 1972, and the last confirmed record was from 1977 when three birds were seen. Intensive studies in 1981 and 1982 failed to find the species, and it is now considered extinct.

THE GOLDEN POISON FROG The golden poison frog or the golden dart frog is endemic to the Pacific coast of Colombia. In the wild the frog is a social animal, living in groups of up to six individuals. Wild specimens of this frog are lethally toxic. This poison dart frog is confirmed to have killed humans who touched the wild frog directly. Like most poison dart frogs, the golden poison frog uses poison only as a self-defense mechanism and not for killing prey.

The average dose of poison carried will vary between locations, and the frogs' consequent local diet, but the average wild golden poison frog is generally estimated to contain about 0.00003 ounce (1 milligram) of poison, enough to kill about 10,000 mice. This dose is enough to kill between 10 and 20 humans. This extraordinarily lethal poison is very rare.

The golden poison frog is a very important frog to the local indigenous cultures, such as the Choco Emberá people in Colombia's rain forest. The frog is the main source of the poison in the darts used by the natives to hunt for food. The Emberá people carefully expose the frog to the heat of a fire, and the frog exudes small amounts of poisonous fluid. The tips of arrows and darts are soaked in the fluid, and keep their lethal effect for more than two years.

NATIONAL FLOWER OF COLOMBIA

The national flower of Colombia is the orchid *Cattleya trianae,* which was named after the Colombian naturalist José Jerónimo Triana. The orchid was selected by the botanist Emilio Robledo, as a representative of the Colombian Academy of History, to determine the most representative flowering plant of Colombia. He described it as one of the most beautiful flowers in the world and selected *Cattleya trianae* as a national symbol.The species grows at 4,921 to 6,562 feet (1,500 to 2,000 m) above sea level, in cloud forests. It is presently an endangered species due to habitat destruction.

Ecotourism is a major factor influencing conservation efforts. Some parks are almost completely undisturbed. Those near cities and along the coasts, however, receive many visitors and need greater care.

AIR POLLUTION

Colombia's climate varies from tropical to temperate, resulting in a diverse environmental system. However, out of Colombia's 44 million people, three-quarters live in the cities. This concentration of people in cities results in urban environmental problems, the most significant of which is air pollution.

In rural areas coffee production, mining activities, and clearing of land for cattle grazing all contribute to deforestation and soil erosion. The exploitation of forests for timber, as well as the prevalence of cocaine trafficking, further intensifies these issues.

Bogotá has more than 8 million inhabitants and is the fifth-biggest city in Latin America. It has more than a million vehicles and a large number of small industries. As a result Bogotá experiences terrible air pollution problems. Seventy percent of the city's air pollution problems stem from automobiles. Traffic is so congested that it can take more than an hour to travel 5 miles (8 km).

The lips of the *Cattleya trianae* orchid is yellow, blue, and red, in the same way as the Colombian flag.

GOVERNMENT EFFORTS

The Colombian government has initiated several programs to protect the environment. By 1959 the Amazon forests, the Andean area, and the Pacific coast were declared protected areas. In 1973 the government created the National Resources and Environment Code. The main environmental agency is the Institute for Development of Renewable Natural Resources and the Environment (INDERENA), established in 1969. Among other activities, it has undertaken extensive projects in the training of personnel in conservation, fishing, and forestry. The Colombian Sanitary Code, in force since January 1982, establishes pollution control standards. In the 2008 Environmental Performance Index (EPI), conducted by U.S. universities Yale and Columbia, Colombia was ranked 9 among 149 countries in the world for environmental protection.

TREATMENT OF BOGOTÁ RIVER

In 2009 a firm received the contract to design upgrades to and expansion of the Salitre Wastewater Treatment Plant in Bogotá, Colombia. This work is part of the Bogotá River Environmental Restoration Project that seeks to transform the Bogotá River from an environmental liability into an urban asset for the metropolitan region by improving the water quality and creating a series of multifunctional parks along the river.

AVAILABILITY OF WATER

The country's estimated coverage of potable water infrastructure reached 97.4 percent of the urban population, providing 90.2 percent of the people with access to sewage systems. In the country's rural areas, the situation is different. Aqueduct service coverage reaches 66 percent of the population, and only 57.9 percent of the rural population has access to a sewer system. Colombia's Water Regulatory Agency estimates that nearly 45 percent of the treated water (by the country's 1,800 water utilities) goes unaccounted for. Water is available and produced, but not paid for by the users, or is lost because of inadequate piping systems. This creates a large problem for utilities and users alike and negatively affects potential future investments. Government sources estimate that the country needs to make environmental investments in the range of $3.3 billion to $3.4 billion per year to maintain an adequate level of protection against all sources of pollution.

OIL IN THE SIERRA NEVADA DE COCUY

The Sierra Nevada de Cocuy is home to important ecosystems. Unfortunately this mountain area also contains oil, the production and export of which Colombia is using to help pay its international debt. Colombia has also agreed to allow the United States, one of its biggest creditors, to explore for oil around the country.

Recycling bins in a park in Colombia.

The U'wa, an indigenous people in the area, have fought hard to preserve their dwindling population (there are only 5,000 of them left) and their shrinking homeland. They believe that oil is the lifeblood of the Earth and that to take oil away is to bleed the Earth dry. Although the Sierra Nevada de Cocuy is thought to contain only 1.5 billion barrels of oil (three months' supply for the United States), there seems to be little choice but to sell this resource, if Colombia is to survive financially. This same story plays out all over the country, as nature and human rights are pitted against international pressure and domestic poverty. Saving the environment in Colombia, as in other parts of the world, is a global issue that concerns all of us.

NATIONAL PARKS AND RESERVES IN COLOMBIA

The protected areas of Colombia are grouped in the National System of Protected Areas. As of 2008 it had 58 natural national parks, which cover about 31,083,459 acres (12,579,081 ha) and represent more than 10 percent of the country's continental land.

LOS KATIOS: A WORLD HERITAGE SITE

Los Katios National Park occupies 278 square miles (720 square km) of land in northwestern Colombia, in northern Chocó, and between the Atrato River and the border with Panama. The reserve contains several different ecosystems. Some 50 percent of Los Katios consists of lowland swamp forests; tropical rain forest covers the other half of the park, ranging from lowlands to mountainous terrain. The area also includes the floodplain of the Atrato River and the foothills of the Darién Mountains in Panama. The Atrato floodplain accounts for 47 percent of Los Katios land and the Darién Mountains make up the other 53 percent. Los Katios merges with the Darién National Park—2,305 square miles (5,970 square km) of land in Panama—to form a massive trans-frontier protected zone.

Los Katios was set aside by the government in 1974 and recognized as a World Heritage Site in 1994. A total of 669 plant species have been found in the reserve, 20 to 25 percent of which are endemic. There are 450 species of birds, representing about 30 percent of all bird species in Colombia. And there are some 550 species of animals in Los Katios, including the manatee, American crocodile, bush dog, giant anteater, and Central American tapir. Los Katios merges with the Darién National Park in Panama, providing a gateway between Central and South America and a habitat for animals from both sides of the border.

Los Katios also protects striking scenery, including the Tendal and Tilupo waterfalls, which measure 82 feet (25 m) and 328 feet (100 m) in height, respectively, and the Ciénagas de Tumaradó swamp, home to the manatee.

One of the problems with environmental conservation in this debt- and conflict-ridden country is that it often directly conflicts with the need to produce for the world market. The country faces intense pressure from world organizations such as the International Monetary Fund and powerful allies such as the United States to open its territory to a variety of industries. Most of these industries cause environmental degradation by polluting or destroying natural habitats. The greatest threat to the park currently is the construction of the Pan-American Highway. The highway will cut through the Atrato River and will act as a barrier to migratory flow and affect the dispersal of aquatic and terrestrial fauna. However the greatest problem associated with highway construction is increased colonization from farmers in Cacarica.

CHIRIBIQUETE NATIONAL PARK Chiribiquete National Natural Park is the largest national park in Colombia. This protected area occupies 4,942 square miles (12,800 square km) of the Amazon region of Colombia. The centerpiece of the protected area is the Chiribiquete Mountains, which form the western edge of the Guiana Shield.

PROPOSED AREAS FOR NATIONAL PARKS Other proposed areas for national parks include the Serranía de Minas Fauna and Flora Sanctuary located near the Puracé National Park in the Department of Huila.

La Serranía de Minas is located within the Cordillera Central mountain range of the Andes, within the municipalities of Saladoblanco, Oporapa, Tarqui, La Plata, El Pital and La Argentina, covering an area of approximately 247,105 acres (100,000 ha). The mountainous ecosystem extends from the municipality of Saladoblanco toward the northeast covering the municipalities of La Argentina, Oporapa, Tarqui, Pital, and La Plata, ending at the municipality of El Agrado. The highest mountain peaks reach up to 8,530 feet (2,600 m).

INTERNET LINKS

www.rff.org/rff/News/Features/Environmental-Management-in-Colombia.cfm

This website covers Colombia's primary conservation efforts.

www.colombialink.com/01_INDEX/index_colombia_eng/index_colombia_04.html

This site provides detailed information about the environment of Colombia.

www.guardian.co.uk/environment/gallery/2008/may/21/endangeredhabitats.forests

This website provides information on how Colombia's cocaine trade is damaging the environment and includes breathtaking pictures.

COLOMBIANS

Young Colombian girls dressed in *La Pollera*, or traditional Colombian dress consisting of a round-necked, lace-edged blouse and a wide, flowery skirt.

6

The country
has a diverse
population
that reflects
Colombia's
colorful history
and the people
who have
inhabited it from
ancient times
to the present.

COLOMBIA'S ETHNIC MAKEUP IS as diverse as its topography. The population descends mainly from three racial groups: Amerindian, African, and European, specifically Spanish. Because objective ethnic classification is impossible, the national census ceased reporting population figures by ethnic group in 1919.

With no official statistics available, a rough estimate of the ethnic composition of the population of almost 46 million is: 58 percent mestizo, or Indigenous-Spanish; 20 percent Caucasian; 14 percent mulatto; 7 percent African or African-Indigenous; and 1 percent Indigenous.

Although ethnic characteristics are important to the people of Colombia, they do not carry the same significance as in the United States. Nonetheless many Colombians continue to identify themselves according to their ancestry and sociocultural status. The various groups are still found in concentrations that reflect patterns set up by the colonial social system. For example indigenous groups that survived the Spanish conquest are found in scattered clusters, isolated from other ethnic groups, in remote areas such as the Guajira Peninsula. Mestizos, who were peasants in earlier times, live mainly in the highlands, where the Spanish conquistadors mingled with the indigenous women. In recent years, however, many mestizos have migrated to the cities and have become members of the urban working class.

A woman from the Kuna Indian tribe. The indigenous Indian groups west of the Magdalena River were virtually wiped out by the Spaniards. Those that have survived live in small groups and keep to themselves.

Afro-Colombians and mulattos who have not joined the urban migration trend continue to live mainly along the coasts and in the foothills of the cordilleras, where there are few Indigenous. Caucasians live predominantly in the cities.

INDIGENOUS GROUPS

A variety of native Indian cultures flourished in Colombia before the 16th century and the arrival of the Europeans. The Quimbaya people inhabited the western slopes of the Cordillera Central. Skilled craftsmen of this group made elaborate necklaces, rings, breastplates, and nose ornaments. They fashioned these items by pouring molten gold into wax molds. They got their inspiration from nature and shaped their gilded works of art in the form of eagles and owls. Quimbaya craftsmen also made many ornaments from clay.

The Chibchas made up almost one-third of the pre-Columbian population. They called themselves *Muisca*, but the Spaniards referred to them as *Chibcha*, which meant "people" in the Muisca language. They lived mainly in the Cundinamarca Basin, which is where Bogotá is today.

The Chibchas developed an advanced and complex civilization. They were deeply religious people, who lived in villages and organized themselves along class lines. Rank and status were inherited through one's mother. To show one's position in society, both men and women often painted their bodies with various designs.

The Chibchas had an efficient system of communal land laws. None of their land was privately owned, and they divided themselves into groups that occupied distinct provinces. Each territory was ruled by a local chief, who reported to a more powerful cacique, or chieftain. Caciques reported to one of the two supreme leaders.

The Chibchas were very skilled in farming, mining, and metal craft. They grew mainly corn, beans, and potatoes, and mined salt, which they traded for other minerals. Although the Chibchas considered salt most valuable, they had an immense fortune in emeralds and gold. Many personal valuables were buried with the dead, but fortunately others have survived to the present and can be seen in Bogotá's Museo del Oro.

The indigenous culture in modern Colombia evolved from the Quimbaya, Chibcha, and Carib groups. There are still a good number of indigenous groups, many living in the eastern two-thirds of the country. Some remain isolated, such as the Motilón, who resist all contact with outsiders. This group has been known in recent times to perch in mountain retreats and attack missionary groups or oil company employees with poisoned arrows and blowguns.

Another indigenous group still found practicing a traditional lifestyle in Colombia is the Yagua Indians of the Amazonian jungle. There are approximately 3,000 Yagua Indians, making their living as hunters and fishermen. They live in huts on stilts that protect them from floods brought by torrential rains.

In groups such as the Chimilas and the Sanha of the Sierra Nevada de Santa Marta mountain region, men and boys live in a temple, where they spin cotton and weave cloth, whereas women and girls live in houses with thatched roofs.

A Makuna Indian family. Despite a rigid social structure, the various ethnic groups live in harmony. Indigenous Indians in urban areas have adapted to more modern lifestyles.

SOCIAL SYSTEM

The massive urban migration that began in the 1950s saw a middle class emerge, resulting in a three-class system: upper, middle, and lower. The upper class, which includes 20 percent of the population, accounts for about 75 to 80 percent of the gross national product. Within this class there is an elite referred to as the "oligarchy" that enjoys wealth and financial security, political power, and education. This group may be considered a caste, since membership is largely due to birthright, not to individual ability.

The emergence in the 20th century of a fairly large middle class paralleled the development of urban society and of the modern institutions of government, education, and social services. The expansion of the government bureaucracy provided a number of positions for the middle class. Teachers were usually included in the middle class, as were most military officers, most of the clergy, and some intellectuals, artists, journalists, and musicians. Owners of medium-sized farms make up most of the rural middle class.

A mestizo family in Colombia. Mestizos identify with Caucasians and have adopted Western styles of dress.

The lower class is composed of the illiterate and the impoverished people who live on the margin of subsistence and possess little or no security, skill, or stable employment. These people reside on the sociopolitical periphery of the society and maintain their traditional way of life; most of their energies are consumed by the struggle for survival.

Other factors that differentiate the classes are lifestyle, education, family background, and occupation. Education is generally considered the key to upward social mobility.

CAUCASIANS Because of the social ranking that was established during colonial times, fair skin became associated with being Spanish and, therefore, helped give those who had it high status.

Today Caucasians continue to hold the highest positions in government and business in Colombian society. Having always been a minority in Colombia, Caucasians follow European lifestyles and behavior and the teachings of the Catholic Church. Their artificial sense of superiority influenced all of society.

Caucasian Colombians still emphasize the importance of intellectual pursuits, and they encourage genteel and creative activities and professions that are possible for a class that has the time and financial security to enjoy these pursuits.

The highest concentration of Afro-Colombians and mulattos is in Chocó, where the first Africans arrived.

Careers in business and industry are considered very acceptable for those who are not from the wealthiest and most prestigious families. However, the importance of ethnic purity varies from region to region and may not matter as much as an old and respected Spanish surname.

MESTIZOS Ethnic mixing began in Colombia from the earliest years, and Colombians often refer to themselves as a mestizo or mixed nation. Approximately 60 percent of the population is of mixed origin, and these people are found in all social classes, occupations, and regions. One of the most unifying factors within this group is the general perception that the status of mestizo or mulatto is better than that of indigenous Indian or Afro-Colombian. Another interesting sociological factor is that mestizos are said to identify with the dominant Caucasian group.

AFRO-COLOMBIANS The Afro-Colombian population density reflects the distribution patterns of the colonial period. Most live in the lowland areas on the Pacific and Atlantic coasts and along the Cauca and Magdalena rivers. In Chocó, Afro-Colombians and mulattos represent 80 percent of the population.

The Afro-Colombian groups in Chocó are quite distinctive in their music, marital practices, and funeral rites. Their distinctive music, more than any

Few Afro-Colombians have become prominent on the national scene. Many Colombians consider the awful living conditions of Afro-Colombians in Buenaventura a national disgrace.

As the Pilgrims crossed the Atlantic Ocean on the Mayflower to reach the New World, the Seaflower, a sister ship, headed for San Andrés Island. The English Puritans settled on the island. These early settlers were replaced by buccaneers who preyed upon Spanish ships, and later by the Spanish. After the famous English pirate Henry Morgan wrested the island from the Spanish, it remained largely uninhabited for more than 100 years. In fact, in 1780, a visitor from the United States reported that only 12 families were living on San Andrés.

In 1822 the islands of San Andrés and nearby Providencia came under Colombian rule. Since then they have become a steady supplier of coconut to the United States and a popular vacation spot for Colombians and many North Americans.

Although these glittering islands have belonged to Colombia for more than a century and a half, the inhabitants have maintained their isolation so well that they have not even adopted the Spanish language or embraced the national religion, Roman Catholicism. These islanders retain the Protestant religion, continue to speak English, and regard themselves as a distinct group from mainland Colombians.

other element, keeps Chocoan Africans very aware of their identity. Many Chocoan-African men are polygamous, which means that they are married to, or live with, more than one woman.

Funeral rites in this region continue for nine days and include night prayers, heavy drinking of alcohol, and gambling. These practices are cultural remnants of their African slave heritage. Their activities reinforce a sense of identity among the Afro-Colombians in the region.

DRESS

Colombian city dwellers dress in the same style as people in the cities of the United States. Colombian youths are eager to follow fashion trends. They wear molas, or embroidered shirts, as frequently as they wear designer jeans and shirts. Climate influences attire. In warm areas on the Pacific coast, men seldom wear coats. There is a rough correlation between the size of the city and the elegance of dress. People in Bogotá, when the climate is cool and damp, have been referred to as *currutacos* (coo-roo-TAH-kos), or dandies, in part because of their finery.

Colombians in the countryside sew most of their own clothing. The basic rural garments include the poncho, ruana, and *bayetón* (bah-yay-TOHN). Each of these garments is a cloak with a hole in the center for the wearer's head to pass through. The garments hang from front to back, leaving the arms free. *Bayetones* are nearly ankle length; ruanas, the most commonly worn of the three, are shawls that hang to a little below the waist, and ponchos fall between the other two lengths.

Among the poor, ruanas are also used as blankets. Woolen ruanas are remarkably waterproof because of the natural oils left in the material. The *pañolón* (PAN-nyah-LOHN) is a traditional women's garment that resembles the ruana. The *pañolón* shawl is customarily made from silk or cotton.

Footwear is an indicator of status. Typical shoes are fiber slippers and sandals. Many rural people prefer to work barefoot. In some groups it is also regarded as ostentatious to wear shoes. However, with rapid urbanization, these customs are fast becoming extinct.

Ruanas are worn by both men and women and can double as blankets.

In the cooler climate of the Andes Mountains, both men and women wear woolen ruanas (capes). Middle- and upper-class women wear stylish versions of the ruana. The most primitive ruanas are made from undyed wool in shades of brown. More stylish versions may be striped or plain, using a wide range of colors.

INTERNET LINKS

www.everyculture.com/wc/Brazil-to-Congo-Republic-of/Colombians. html

This site provides a good summary of Colombian culture.

www.ediplomat.com/np/cultural_etiquette/ce_co.htm

This site contains an excellent overview of the cultural etiquette of Colombia.

http://gosouthamerica.about.com/od/colregcoasts/p/SanAndres.htm

This site provides a touristic overview of San Andrés Island.

LIFESTYLE

The bustling streets of the financial district in Bogotá. In the streets of Colombian towns, like those in other towns in the world, one can see all sorts of people, from well-dressed office workers to street vendors.

7

LIFESTYLE VARIES BY REGION IN Colombia. In Leticia, Colombia's southernmost city, inhabitants depend on trapping and fishing for their livelihood. Even when they meet in the town square, Leticia residents must be wary of the hazards that may be encountered in the heart of the jungle, because Leticia lies in the Amazonian valley.

Colombia is a contradiction when it comes to lifestyle. Nearly half of its population (49.2 percent) lives below the poverty line, yet it ranks among the top 10 happiest countries in the world in the Happy Planet Index.

Fishing boats docked by a riverside in Colombia.

A Guambino market in Cauca.

On the llanos, vaqueros, or cowboys, drive their herds all day in the areas where much of the country's meat and grain is produced. Wearing traditional straw hats, they tether cattle and tend mules, pigs, goats, chickens, sheep, and other livestock.

Fishing villages and harbors thrive along the coasts, where the inhabitants rely on the ocean for their livelihood. Men work on the docks shirtless, loading and unloading cargo with bandannas tied around their necks.

In the populated areas of the mountains, the numerous coffee plantations are the main income source. Residents also fish in the clear mountain streams. The typical workday of coffee plantation workers begins around 8:00 A.M. They tie a plastic bucket around their waist, which they fill with coffee beans. When the bucket is full, they empty it into a plastic sack and start filling it again. The workers move very quickly, because they are paid according to the amount they pick. An experienced coffee picker handles about 110 pounds (50 kg) of beans each day. After working continuously for four hours, the workers take their sacks full of coffee beans to the plantation manager, who measures what has been picked and gives the workers their wages for the day.

City dwellers work city jobs. There are accountants, doctors, lawyers, office staff, janitors, and many other occupations, as in cities throughout the world.

FAMILY LIFE

The family is a very important social unit in Colombia. When Colombians refer to the family, they mean a wide circle of kinship that consists of several generations—what a North American would probably think of as the extended family.

The ideal of the family as a close-knit unit is still very much present in all social and ethnic groups in Colombia.

The function and structure of the family does vary, though, depending on regional and socioeconomic factors. Typically children live with their families until they marry and often even afterward. Young adults from upper-middle-class and upper-class families often get their own apartments before marriage, but it is still quite common for newly married couples to live with their large families until they have saved enough money to start their own home.

Family ties are somewhat weaker in urban centers than in rural areas, but households are usually large regardless of locality. Grandparents and other aging relatives are customarily part of the household, in addition to the core family unit of mother, father, and children. Cousins and their relatives can also join the family circle for extended periods of time when necessary. The setup is usually flexible. Only the rural upper class has traditional patriarchal domiciles, in which married sons and their families remain in the home.

Sunday is a family day. Colombians are likely to visit their families on this day, for the importance of kinship is greatly emphasized. It is the basis of much social and business interaction.

The family also plays a significant role in the Colombian business world. There are many family-run businesses in which few, if any, positions of importance are given to outsiders. Employers feel safe in hiring family members, believing that the relatives' true strengths and weaknesses are well known among the family. In short there are no surprises from the new employee. Furthermore a sense of family loyalty motivates employees to keep their bosses' best interests at heart.

Local children accompanying their grandfather at his shop.

Among the lower socioeconomic groups, household membership and the structure of the family can be considerably different from those of middle- and upper-class families. The reason for this is that formal marriage may not be the foundation of the family relationship. Sometimes the father is not a permanent resident in the home, and the mother becomes the chief authority in the family. This trend is most prevalent in Chocó, where, in the 1960s, about one-third of households were headed by women.

Extended family ties are often weakened in the lower-class family by the ever-increasing need to migrate to urban centers to find employment. But in keeping with Hispanic uniformity in family life, rural migrants will move to areas where other relatives have previously relocated, and the pattern of extended-family living is resumed.

Family background and name are most important to those who move up the social ladder. Colombia's most respected families are descended from 16th-century Spanish settlers. The families with this distinction proudly display crests above the doors of their homes. A sense of pride is kept alive by a tradition of telling stories about the lives and deeds of their ancestors.

COMPADRAZGO

Kinship ties are stretched even further by a traditional Hispanic relationship known as *compadrazgo* (kom-pah-DRAHS-go), a spiritual bond linked to Catholic notions of baptismal godparenthood. In this relationship, social and emotional bonds are created when a godparent accepts serious responsibilities for a child's welfare, and in turn, earns great respect from the child. Furthermore a spiritual bond is created between the child's parents and godparents.

Although children refer to their godfather and godmother as *padrino* (pah-DREE-no) and *madrina* (mah-DREE-nah), respectively, their parents usually address the godparents as *compadre* (kom-PAH-dray) and *comadre*

(kom-MAH-dray), signifying both friendship and companionship, and acknowledging the importance of the parent-godparent bond.

Colombians may have several sets of godparents, chosen at various important milestones in their lives. But the baptismal godparents are far the most important. They often supervise the religious education of the child, and it is not unusual for an orphaned child to be adopted by his or her baptismal godparents.

The godparent relationship is not limited to Colombians of Hispanic descent. Chibcha Indian godparents are involved in rituals such as earlobe piercing, the first clipping of fingernails, and the first cutting of hair. The godfathers who cut the child's hair are said to be the most honored.

Extended families are a feature of Colombian life. In certain regions, households are headed by women, since the men may not always live in the home.

DATING AND MARRIAGE

Dating without chaperones has recently become more common in Colombia, especially among educated families in the cities. Young Colombians develop exclusive relationships rather quickly, and they regard their counterparts in the United States as promiscuous because of the tendency to "play the field."

Most Colombians go through formal marriage ceremonies. However, where indigenous and Afro-Colombian influence is strong, people usually practice trial marriage. Many communities openly acknowledge this as a legitimate pre-matrimonial stage. Civil marriage has been legal in Colombia since 1973. Before that only Catholic marriages were valid for Catholics. Nonetheless many Colombians feel that there is less commitment to civil marriages and thus look down on them. Catholic marriages are viewed as the ideal and as the legal, social, and sexual basis of the family.

Religious marriage also connotes social status, and many Colombians see marriage as a path to social mobility. Parents are always hopeful that their young daughters will marry a man of great status and wealth. But upper-class Colombians are reluctant to wed persons of a lower social status. Matchmaking is not uncommon among the aristocracy, with a second or third cousin often being the chosen match.

GENDER ROLES

The word *macho* is used a lot in the United States, but its meaning is rarely clear. *Machismo*, or being macho, is actually a Hispanic concept that distinguishes masculine attributes. It provides a guideline for men to follow, and the term does not have the negative connotation that it has in the United States.

To Latin Americans a macho man is one who is strong, respected, protective, and capable of providing for his wife and family. Although aggressiveness is something that North Americans associate with being macho, Colombian men vary in their aggressiveness, according to social class. In general middle- and upper-class men tend to be less aggressive than men in the lower classes.

Colombian women, too, aspire to a socially approved image, and much emphasis is placed on being feminine. This desired image can be seen in the way Colombian women dress. The women of Bogotá, *bogotanas* (bog-o-TAN-nas), dress fashionably and wear makeup even when they are running errands or just staying around the house. This feminine image is so prevalent that travel guides list the beautiful women of Cali as one of the city's main attractions!

FAMILY ROLES

Many Colombians live with their children, parents, grandparents, and other relatives under one roof, and each family member has a role to play in the extended household.

Traditionally the father was considered the head of the family, and the mother had full responsibility for preparing meals, doing household chores, and taking care of the children. However, Colombian society is changing, and new family arrangements are arising. The old "macho" man and maternal woman stereotypes are giving way to new gender roles within the modern family. For example more Colombian women— especially in the middle classes—are finding jobs outside the home and contributing to the family income, whereas Colombian men are learning to communicate with their children.

Until recently women of the upper class were not allowed to work outside the home. The only acceptable activity was charitable volunteer work. Even social activities were limited to school and the home, and women were chaperoned at parties. Now many upper-class women are well educated and enjoy careers in a variety of fields including high political office. More legal rights have been granted to women, and their participation and involvement in public affairs, government, and higher education is increasing.

Limitations have always been greater for middle- and lower-class women. It has generally been an economic requirement for these wives to work out in the fields alongside their husbands or to be employed outside the home and contribute their paychecks to the family budget. Unfortunately wages remain low for these women.

A farmer and his wife stand hand in hand on their porch in Colombia.

THE WORK WEEK

There are 18 national holidays in Colombia each year, 12 of which are religious. The six secular public holidays are New Year's Day (January 1), Labor Day (May 1), Independence Day (July 20), Battle of Boyacá Day (August 7),

MARKET DAYS

Although rural life involves a lot of hard work, country dwellers do enjoy some recreation. They especially look forward to market days.

One day of the week is designated as market day in a village, and people from miles around come to visit and enjoy the festivities. All modes of transportation are employed, not only to bring produce, animals, and handicrafts to the market but also to transport visitors and customers. Open-air buses packed with passengers are seen on the road next to burros (donkeys) and push carts.

The marketplace is usually located in the main square of the village. Goods and wares are spread out on wooden stands or stacked on the ground. Chickens strut past as people bargain with their friends and neighbors.

Market days are a great opportunity for people in the countryside to meet one another, catch up, and trade in a variety of goods.

Columbus Day (October 12), and Independence of Cartagena Day (November 11). The only day of rest is Sunday. Most Colombians work a 6-day week.

In the industrial centers, the workday begins between 8:00 and 8:30 A.M. and ends between 6:30 and 7:00 P.M. On farms and in the torrid zone, laborers may start work at 6:00 or 7:00 A.M.

Government offices are open from 8:00 A.M. to noon and again from 2:00 to 6:00 P.M. Most businesses operate from 9:00 A.M. to 5:00 P.M., Monday through Friday. Stores are generally open Monday through Saturday, from 9:00 A.M. to 12:30 P.M. and then from 2:00 to 7:00 P.M., though store hours may vary. Banks are open from 9:00 A.M. to 3:00 P.M., Monday through Thursday, and from 9:00 A.M. to 3:30 P.M. on Friday. ATMs may be accessed at any time of the day.

Office workers having a meeting in Colombia. More women are joining the workforce. Some even enter traditionally male professions.

MEETINGS AND VISITS

In Colombia business appointments are made at least a week in advance, and are often reconfirmed beforehand, but people may arrive 15 to 20 minutes late for a business meeting.

Colombia has a tradition of hospitality. People often invite friends to their homes. Relatives are the most frequent visitors in Colombian homes. At social gatherings the host family dresses formally and entertains the guests in the living room.

Supper time ordinarily begins around 8:00 P.M., but when there are guests, everyone dines at 10:00 or 11:00 P.M. Guests are expected to arrive 15 to 30 minutes late. Drinks and snacks are served before the multicourse dinner begins.

EDUCATION

Colombia spends very little of the national GDP on education. Nonetheless free education is available to all, and the adult literacy rate is 93 percent.

There is still the perception among Colombians that private education is superior to public education. Wealthier Colombians prefer to send their children to private schools, and it is also common for middle-class children to attend private schools. Schools in Colombia are called either *escuelas* (es-coo-AY-las) or *colegios* (co-LAY-he-os).

Despite an increase in government spending on education, some problems remain in the public education system. In the countryside, for example, there are sometimes not enough seats available in the schools.

School is compulsory for all Colombian children between the ages of 5 and 16 years. However education is not always a priority among the poorest families. For them the money that the children can earn from work is needed to support the household.

The Cartagena University tower in Colombia.

To qualify for higher education, all students must sit for a state test. The examination board is the Colombian Institute for the Promotion of Higher Education.

NURSERY SCHOOL Most children over one year old are provided with daycare and nursery school in community homes sponsored by the National Institute for Family Welfare, where mothers from the community take care of their own children, as well as the children from the immediate neighborhood. When children in Colombia learn how to read and write, they are usually transferred to the elementary school.

ELEMENTARY Free elementary education consists of two years of kindergarten and five years of elementary school. Entering into secondary school is dependent on completion of the elementary program.

HIGH SCHOOL High school programs take six years to complete. Students can then be admitted to an institute of higher education.

VOCATIONAL HIGH school programs are assuming a vocational focus. This change is intended to prepare students to meet the country's need for skilled labor in both agriculture and industry. This new emphasis is a real change from previous patterns of education that concentrated on preparing high school students to enter colleges and universities. Technical degrees usually take three years to complete.

COLLEGE More than 320,000 students, some of them from the working class, attend 73 universities in Colombia. Most university degrees take five years to complete. There are perhaps another 60 additional institutions of higher education in the country.

Because of the challenging terrain and overwhelming poverty, often there is no way for children to get to school, and education by radio and television has been very successful. Colombia was the first South American country to use radio for this purpose. Rural people gather around a radio that is set up in a public place, and lessons in reading, writing, history, and geography are transmitted over the airwaves. Television was added to the rural educational system in the early 1980s to reach all areas of the country in a more contemporary and effective manner.

In some rural areas teachers are poorly qualified and dropout rates are high. In urban areas, on the other hand, teachers are generally better prepared and knowledgeable.

Kindergarten children on an excursion. Private kindergartens with good facilities are available but admission costs to these schools are too expensive for average families.

HOUSING

Housing in Colombia is designed in different styles and built from different materials, based on the climate in the location and the income level of the occupant. Classic colonial mansions and modern ranch-style houses can be found in the cities and suburbs, whereas on the outskirts stand the most desperate slums, where unemployment, poverty, and crime are rampant. In the rural areas a large ranch of an upper-class family may be located near the small landholding of a subsistence farmer.

In remote areas people live in bamboo or thatched *tambos* (TAM-bos), which are built on stilts that hold the structure about 6 feet (1.8 m) above the land or water. In swampy areas the stilts keep the water from getting into the house, and in dry regions, they protect the occupants from snakes, insects, and other dangerous wildlife. One of the stilts is notched to enable the occupants to climb up into the house.

Inadequate housing, overcrowding, and insufficient utilities such as water and sanitation are all contributors to the housing problem in Colombia. More than 11.5 million homes in Colombia do not satisfactorily meet the basic necessities of the families that live in them. More than 40 percent of that figure represents inadequate housing and overcrowding, whereas another 20 percent demonstrates problems with public utilities. Alarmingly in 1990, 30 percent of housing in Medellín consisted of illegal settlements in steep, hillside, peripheral communities. These housed approximately half of the city's growing population, and this trend has not changed much over time. Medellín is surrounded by mountains in nearly all directions and has no means of spreading out. However, urban housing in Medellín is undergoing a boom, with an increasing demand for apartments as the Colombian economy grows.

AT HOME IN BOGOTÁ

Houses in Bogotá tend to form a solid wall facing the sidewalk. There are no side yards, and neighbors cannot speak to one another over a fence, because the rear patio is surrounded by a high wall.

The typical home has two floors and no basement. The windows on the first floor are striped by iron bars or ornamental grillwork for security. Most modern homes have a patio in the back. Part of this patio is a garden, usually accessible from the living or dining room.

Most homes also have a maid's quarters with direct access to the kitchen, garage, and service patio. The location of the maid's quarters facilitates her work. Traditionally the maid is responsible for the first-floor chores—cooking in the kitchen, washing and ironing on the patio, and accepting deliveries through the garage. The lady of the house, the señora, tends to the chores upstairs, where the bedrooms and bathrooms are located. She spends a lot of time upstairs in the bedroom, even entertaining her women friends there. The living room is seldom used, and the family often congregates in the upstairs hallway.

In La Candelaria, Bogotá's old section, houses form a solid wall facing the street.

INTERNET LINKS

http://journals.worldnomads.com/safetyhub/country/48/Colombia

This site contains beautiful pictures and information about Medellín.

www.lonelyplanet.com/colombia/bogota

This website includes beautiful photos and informative socio-cultural facts about Bogotá.

www.mapsofworld.com/colombia/society-and-culture/family.html

This site provides a good summary of how the family unit functions in Colombia.

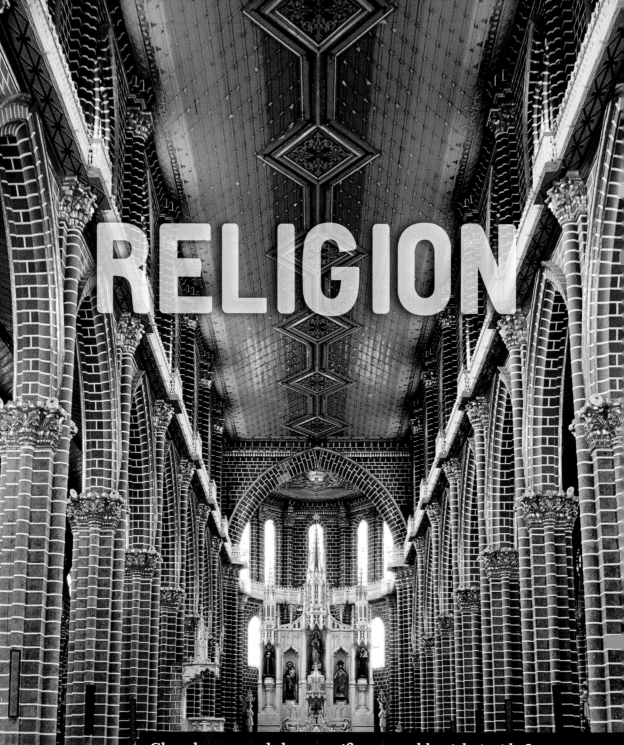

RELIGION

Church pews and the magnificent marble aisle inside La Basílica menor de la Inmaculada Concepción in Jardin, Antioquia.

8

THE COLOMBIAN CONSTITUTION guarantees freedom of worship. Roman Catholicism has been the established religion in Colombia since the 1500s. The Church in Colombia is known as one of the most conservative and traditional in Latin America.

There has long been a great emphasis in Colombia's Catholic Church on the formal aspects of the faith, and most Colombians regularly observe holy days, attend Mass, and receive the sacraments.

Catholic churches are the biggest, most imposing buildings in all Colombian towns. The parish church is the center of activity in most communities, and Colombian churches serve some of the largest Mass congregations in Latin America.

The primary cathedral of Bogotá in Plaza Bolívar.

CHURCH AND STATE

The constitution of 1886 gave a special status to the Catholic Church, and the concordat of 1887 between the Pope and the Colombian government defined a special role for the Church in civil matters. However, in 1853, Colombia was the first Latin American country to pass a law separating church and state. The concordat and constitution remained in effect until 1973, when a new concordat was issued. The Church lost its influence in education, in the territories occupied by indigenous people, and in marriage regulation. The Colombian constitution of 1991 abolished the previous condition of the Roman Catholic Church as the official church, and it included two articles providing for freedom of worship.

However, the Church still has a profound political influence and its close alliance with wealthy Conservatives has sparked debate about its traditional role and majority appeal.

The oldest religious structure in Mérida, the Iglesia del Carmen church is an architectural marvel, as well as a seat of the Carmelite Brotherhood.

OTHER FAITHS

Although 80 percent of the population is Catholic, some 13.5 percent of the population belongs to non-Catholic forms of Christianity, 2 percent are agnostic, and the remaining 4.5 percent belong to other groups, such as Islam and Judaism. There are local Baha'i spiritual assemblies and synagogues for more than 10,000 Jews in the country. Indian tribal religions are practiced by a number of lowlands and jungle groups, including the Arhuaco, Coreguaje, Cuna, Kogua, Guajiro, Macu, Barasano, and Tatuyo.

INDIVIDUAL FAITH AND PRACTICE

In 1970 a general survey in Colombia found that 63 percent of Catholics attended Mass at least once a week, 67 percent prayed daily, and only 24 percent did not pray at all. This represented a marked difference from results obtained in 1960, when only 10 percent were said to fulfill these minimum requirements of Catholicism. Since then there was a resurgence of conservative worship.

Carved offerings pasted on the wall of the Las Lajas sanctuary.

Although many people in the urban areas only attend Mass on religious holidays, their beliefs and values remain faithful to religious teachings. Major family events such as birth and baptism, marriage, and death are usually celebrated in church.

An important role of religious organizations is to run basic institutions in society, such as schools and hospitals. There are more than 120 different religious orders, institutes, and lay organizations running hundreds of primary and secondary schools, hospitals, clinics, orphanages, colleges, and eight universities. The best known of these are Pontificia Universidad Javeriana (in Cali) and Pontificia Universidad Javeriana (in Bogotá), both Jesuit universities.

RELIGIOUS HOLIDAYS

Of Colombia's 18 national holidays, 12 are religious, specifically Catholic. Easter and Christmas are the most important. The remaining 10 are Epiphany (January 6), Saint Joseph's Day (March 19), Maundy Thursday, Good Friday, Ascensión (43 days after Easter Sunday), Corpus Christi, Saints Peter and Paul Day (June 29), Assumption Day (August 15), All Saints' Day (November 1), and Immaculate Conception Day (December 8).

THE KOGUA TRIBAL RELIGION

The Kogua are Colombian Indians who live on the slopes of the Sierra Nevada de Santa Marta. This farming group of 5,000 treasures its ancestral lore about the laws of nature and the governance of the universe. The Kogua high priest, or Máma, contemplates the skies, because true knowledge for the Kogua is knowledge of the laws of Mother Nature. For them living in harmony with these laws is the key to the preservation of the universe.

The high priest is responsible for watching over the universe, as well as watching over the spiritual and social order of the group. He knows the Kogua belief in the nine-stage creation of the universe. This knowledge, combined with the laws of nature, means the Kogua believe that they alone hold the secret of what causes the sun to rise each morning and what determines the way things are born and mature, multiply, and die.

CATHEDRALS

A number of notable places of worship can be found in Colombia, most of them dating back to colonial days. One cathedral that is somewhat unusual is in a salt mine in Zipaquirá. It was carved from salt by the miners, and as many as 15,000 people can congregate in its immense gallery. The 75-foot-high (23-m-high) ceiling arches above a 20-ton (18-metric-ton) block of salt that serves as the main altar.

The Church of San Francisco in Popayán has a bell that can be heard throughout the valley. In its pulpit is a gracefully carved figure of a Creole (person of Spanish descent born in the New World) girl carrying a basket of fruit atop her head. The altarpiece carving of the Virgin of the Immaculate Conception is also very impressive. Outside the church stand simple stone carvings in contrast to the intricate carvings within.

Cartagena's cathedral, located in the Plaza de Bolívar, has a fortress-like exterior that was completed in the early 1600s. While under construction, the cathedral was partially destroyed by the cannons of Sir Francis Drake, the English seaman and adventurer. Spain and England were at war at that time. Alterations were made to the cathedral, covering it in stucco, by the archbishop of Cartagena in the early 20th century.

Other beautiful churches include *La Ermita* (The Hermitage), a splendid Gothic-style church located in Cali. The Carmelita Church in Medellín is another outstanding example of Spanish colonial architecture.

The Cathedral of Zipaquirá is located in a most unexpected place. Two hours north of Bogotá, the cathedral is built inside a huge salt mine!

INTERNET LINKS

www.spainexchange.com/guide/CO-religion.htm

This site provides a concise overview of religion in Colombia.

www.colombia.travel/en/international-tourist/vacations-holidays-where-to-go/recommended-weekend-destinations/zipaquira-salt-cathedral

This beautiful site features the Zipaquirá Salt Cathedral, named the first wonder of Colombia.

www.hispanic-culture-online.com/christmas-in-colombia.html

This website contains lovely pictures that depict what it means to celebrate Christmas in Colombia.

LANGUAGE

Colombia has a long press history. Newsstands carry local as well as international papers and magazines.

9

SPANISH IS THE DOMINANT language in Colombia. It is also the official language of the country. Colombians take pride in their use of language and have been said to preserve the purest use of Spanish in Latin America.

Although there is remarkable ethnic diversity in the country, only about 4 percent of the population speaks an indigenous language. Of these many speak Spanish as well. The inhabitants of the San Andrés and Providencia islands speak primarily English, which they inherited from the English Puritans who settled in these islands in the 17th century.

Colombia has a rich diversity of languages—80 of them in all.

A book vendor in his market stall in Cali. Colombians frequently visit bookstores and book fairs.

Regional accents differentiate the speech of Colombians living in different areas. The most distinguishable accent is heard on the Caribbean coast, where the spoken Spanish sounds more like the Spanish spoken in the Dominican Republic or in Cuba than like that in Bogotá, Bucaramanga, or Medellín.

NONVERBAL COMMUNICATION

There are not many differences between the gestures and the nonverbal behavior of Colombians and North Americans, but there are a few worth mentioning. Colombians gesture for people to come toward them in a manner similar to the North American wave, with the palm facing up. They indicate height in two ways. When describing an animal, they hold the hand as though it were resting on the animal's head. When describing a person, they hold the hand as though it were behind rather than above the person's head.

Etiquette is important. "Body language" taboos include entertaining a visitor barefoot, putting one's feet up on a desk or chair, slouching in a chair, yawning in public, and eating on the street.

Generally Colombians who live in cities away from the coast are quite formal. They tend to express themselves verbally more than through movement and gestures. In Bogotá, for instance, the locals rarely use excited gestures or raise their voices when conveying their feelings or ideas. Their formality often keeps them from explicitly expressing their anger.

Pretending not to hear or giving a slow response to an unwelcome question would be typical ways for inland Colombians to express their anger. Because of their formality, foreigners often perceive Colombians—especially those in Bogotá—as distant or cold. Residents of the coastal areas, however, tend to be more expressive nonverbally.

GREETINGS

Greetings are an important part of Colombian etiquette. A verbal greeting is almost always accompanied by at least a handshake. Men shake hands with both women and men. Women sometimes shake hands with other women, frequently while grasping each other's right forearm. Close female friends often kiss one another on the cheek. Relatives or close male friends may hug.

Once first contact is accomplished, the greeting ritual continues with polite questioning about the well-being of each other's family members. Only then, after some small talk, is it appropriate to discuss business.

There are also procedures to follow when entering a group. Everyone must be greeted, at the very least with eye and verbal contact, and preferably with a handshake. It is also essential to say good-bye to everyone when leaving the group.

FORMS OF ADDRESS

When addressing someone, Colombians can use the familiar *tú* (too) or the formal *usted* (oos-TED), both meaning "you." In certain regions, Colombians also use alternative forms, such as the antiquated *su merced* in Boyacá and the very intimate *vos* in the Valle del Cauca. There are no exact guidelines. Among social equals, *usted* is used, but it changes to *tú* as the people get to know one another better. Persons of higher social status or those who are older may ask others to address them using *tú*, but Colombians may feel uncomfortable using the intimate form of address with persons of higher status. It is clearly not a simple matter!

Use of first names is equated with using *tú*—that is, with intimacy. Before acquaintances have reached a certain familiarity, they address one another as *Señor* and *Señora*.

Colombians hold their hand palm outward as though it were behind the head when demonstrating a child's height.

NEWSPAPERS

Colombia has a free press, and the leading newspapers contain a wide range of international and national news, criticism, and commentary, plus special features.

Newspapers have always been the major source for an accurate picture of the general state of Colombia and a vehicle for political debate. The press has been a part of Colombian culture since 1791, when the first colonial newspaper, *Papel Periódico de la Ciudad de Santa Fe de Bogotá*, was founded.

Sign languages used in Colombia include Colombian Numerals, Colombian Sign Language, and Providence Island Sign Language.

THE SPANISH ALPHABET

The Spanish alphabet looks similar to the English alphabet, but it consists of 27 letters:
a, b, c, d, e, f, g, h, i, j, k, l, m, n, ñ, o, p, q, r, s, t, u, v, w, x, y, z

The letters k and w are generally found only in foreign words that have become part of the Spanish vocabulary. The k sound is represented in Spanish by c before a, o, and u and by qu before e and i. Before 1994 the Spanish alphabet included the letters ch and ll. However, Spanish language academies around the world decided to drop ch and ll as separate letters when alphabetizing. Although old Spanish dictionaries listed words beginning with ch after words beginning with c, most Spanish dictionaries now list words in the same order followed by English dictionaries. Thus words beginning with ch are no longer listed in a separate section but are treated as words beginning with c.

Spanish vowels often have accents, but these accented vowels are not considered separate letters, unlike some other languages. Also, unlike English, each Spanish vowel has one fundamental sound:

a   *as in* mama
e   *as in* check
i   *as in* police
o   *as in* or
u   *as in* rude

Many of the consonants have the same approximate sound as in English, though a linguist would consider these differences significant. Very noticeable distinctions are as follows:

- **b** *and* **v** *are pronounced identically, as a* b.
- **d**, *when it is within a word, is pronounced like the English* th *in* then.
- **s** *is pronounced like the* s *in the English word* son.
- **ll**, *which represents one sound, is a blend of l and y, as in* call you, *or is often simply pronounced like y, as in* yore.
- **h** *is not pronounced in Spanish.*
- **j** *has no exact English equivalent; a throaty* h *sound is the closest English comparison; this would also be the sound for* g *before e and i.*
- **r**, *within a word, is a flapped sound like the* tt *in* kitty.
- **rr** *within a word is similar to the r sound described above; however, it is trilled. (Note that rr is not officially a letter of the alphabet.)*

There is a close relation between the government and the press, even though Colombian journalists generally maintain a strong belief in press freedom. For example, the two leading newspapers in Bogotá, *El Tiempo* and *El Espectador,* are identified with the Liberals, and two others, *La República* and *El Nuevo Siglo*, support the Conservative Party. The most influential conservative paper in the country is *El Colombiano*, which is published in Medellín.

Colombia is one of the most dangerous places in the world for journalists to work. Media workers face intimidation by drug traffickers, guerrillas, and paramilitary groups. More than 120 Colombian journalists were killed in the 1990s, many for reporting on drug trafficking and corruption.

The media-freedom organization Reporters Without Borders has denounced armed groups, corrupt politicians, and drug barons in Colombia as "enemies of press freedom."

Colombians have a strong bias toward the truthfulness of the printed word; television and radio have been regulated by the government throughout the years. As a result, in this class-conscious nation, literacy has held a certain prestige that can be appreciated in this Colombian joke: "The country has two kinds of people, those with 'culture' and those with transistor radios."

Those interested in a more international news perspective can buy the *Miami Herald* in and around Bogotá and the *New York Times*, the *Wall Street Journal, El Pais, and Le Monde* at bookstores and newsstands in major cities.

Rebels have used radio to spread their propaganda. One of the main clandestine stations is the FARC-operated *La Voz de la Resistencia*, which the rebel group has described as another battlefront.

INTERNET LINKS

www.ethnologue.com/show_country.asp?name=CO

This site provides a comprehensive report on the languages of Colombia.

www.spanishdict.com/

This is the world's largest Spanish learning website. One can easily pick up a few phrases here.

www.youtube.com/watch?v=1blXYCHjlDQ&feature=relmfu

This site contains an interesting beginner-level Spanish pronoun lesson.

ARTS

Children playing traditional folk music with various local instruments.

· · · · · · · · · ·

10

Colombian culture
is a complex mix
of European,
African, and
Native American
traditions.

C OLOMBIANS TAKE GREAT PRIDE
in their artistic and cultural
achievements. In fact Bogotá has
been called the "Athens of Latin America,"
in reference to the residents' appreciation
and patronage of the arts. It is said with
great pride that there are more bookstores
lining the streets of the capital city than
restaurants or cafés, and that more poets
than generals have become presidents.

The regionalism caused by Colombia's extreme geographical contrasts
has also had an impact on the country's cultural and artistic life.
Bogotá is best known for its literature and poetry, the Caribbean coast

Beautiful gold treasures crafted by ancient Indians reveal a great mastery of
metalwork techniques.

Gonzalo Jiménez de Quesada (1499—1579), the Spanish conquistador who founded Santa Fé de Bogotá—what is now the city of Bogotá—in 1538, was also a prolific writer. He wrote several chronicles, pieces of descriptive and historical writing that conquistadors and men of letters sent back to Spain to inform the Spanish Crown of their discoveries.

A couple of decades after Jiménez de Quesada's death, Juan Rodríguez Freyle (1566—1640) wrote the first widely read chronicle and exposé of the conquest and settlement of Nueva Granada, which he called El Carnero *(The Ram).*

is famed for its songs and dances, and Cali is known for its salsa dancing and experimental theater. Medellín has produced many important artists and intellectuals. The religious festivals and rituals of the Roman Catholic Church are perhaps the only areas of creative expression shared by all of Colombia's departments, or states.

HISTORICAL BACKGROUND

Colombia's artistic and literary achievements fall into three periods: pre-Hispanic, colonial (when Colombia was a Spanish colony), and republican (after independence from Spain). Although there was an obvious and marked transition from the first to the second era, the change from the colonial period to the republican period was much more gradual.

When the conquistadores arrived in Colombia, they destroyed any traditional Indian arts they encountered and insisted that all Colombian artistic expression be similar to styles and genres that were then popular in Spain. Their dislike for Indian art was evident in paintings and religious sculpture of the colonial period, although some churches built during that time housed indigenous carvings. Most artistic works of the period were reminiscent of the Spanish style.

As the desire for independence grew, the Creoles rejected everything that connected them with Spain, including artistic motifs. However, much of their

There is archaeological evidence of ceramic production on Colombia's Caribbean coast beginning around the year 5940 B.C. around the town of San Jacinto. This would place these pottery shards among the oldest ever recovered anywhere.

inspiration was based on the contemporary artistic modes of other European countries, especially France.

It was only at the beginning of the 20th century that Colombians truly began to appreciate their indigenous artistic heritage, and what had been their mere acknowledgment of Indian monuments and colonial paintings grew into a great source of pride in their heritage and a basis for the creation of modern Colombian art forms.

LITERATURE

The most valuable Spanish contribution to the Colombian arts scene was in language and literature, dating back to Gonzalo Jiménez de Quesada, a lawyer-scholar-explorer. Colombia's first pieces of national literature came from the historical and descriptive writings of this conquistador.

Other leaders, such as Simón Bolívar, Antonio Nariño, and Francisco de Paula Santander, were both gifted writers and students of philosophy and European and American history. The 17th century was considered the Baroque period in Latin American literature. The writing was exaggerated, flowery, and not particularly notable. The following century did not produce

The monument of "The Old Shoes" stands by the roadside in Cartagena in memory of local poet Luis Carlos López.

celebrated works either, which was perhaps a reflection of the decline of Spanish literature generally.

The 19th century, however, marked the beginning of significant Colombian literary output. *Tertulias* (tayr-Too-lee-ahs), or literary salons, began to appear, where patriots discussed forbidden books that were smuggled into the colony. This was the Romantic period in Colombian and world literature, and poetry was the major literary form. The works dealt with love, patriotism, nature, and religion. A leading Colombian religious poet of this time was José Eusebio Caro (1817—53). Character development and a variety of metrical forms marked his works. So much creative energy went into poetry in the 19th century that few outstanding novels emerged.

In 1867 Jorge Isaacs wrote *Maria*, the most widely admired Latin American romantic novel of the 19th century. At the end of the 19th century Colombian poets and authors took part in a new literary movement called *modernismo* (mo-der-NEES-mo), Latin America's first original contribution to world literature. Famous literary figures from the modernist movement included José Asunción Silva (1865—96) and Guillermo Valencia (1873—1943).

Twentieth-century literature focused on realistic social commentary in the form of regional novels. Tomás Carrasquilla (1858—1940) wrote a novel about the mountain people of Antioquia, *The Marquess of Yolombó* (*La Marqueza de Yolombó*); José Eustasio Rivera (1889—1928) dealt with Amazonian life in *La Vorágine* (*The Vortex*).

The 1960s brought a new literary age led by Gabriel García Márquez (born in 1928). His 1967 novel, *Cien Años de Soledad* (*One Hundred Years of*

Colombian writer Gabriel García Márquez won the Nobel Prize for Literature in 1982.

ART THAT REACHES OUT TO PEOPLE

Roldanillo, a rural town of 50,000 inhabitants in the Cauca River Valley, is more than 400 years old. Throughout its history, most of its sons have lived by farming and cattle raising—except Omar Rayo (born in 1928), an artist of world renown and the force behind Roldanillo's imaginative Rayo Museum for Latin American Prints and Drawings.

Nearly hidden in the center of the peaceful and traditional town, the museum is a strikingly beautiful collection of eight one-room spaces that are naturally lit by glass-domed ceilings. The museum is devoted to works on paper and is the only one of its kind in Latin America.

Rayo has been living in New York in self-exile since 1960, but his commitment to his birthplace has inspired him to return and share his art. The museum is not, however, merely an exhibition of his works. It is a workshop-museum where lithography, photography, and photoengraving are also taught. Other artists exhibit at the Rayo Museum as well as teach and create new pieces.

In conjunction with the museum, there is also an exhibit on the highway leading from Cali to Roldanillo that displays on billboards works by 19 artists, including Fernando Botero and Mario Toral. The highway museum, called Arte Vial, brings art out into the street to be viewed by all, even those who do not visit museums. It is the hope of Omar Rayo that young people in rural areas will now have the opportunity to become increasingly aware of the beauty of modern art through Arte Vial and the Rayo Museum.

Solitude), is one of the most widely read novels in the Spanish language since Cervantes's *Don Quixote*. Many novelists have imitated his style, employing magical realism, emphasizing social problems and the government's inability to solve them.

VISUAL ARTS

Colombian visual art borrowed Spanish techniques and themes and received little attention until the 19th century, when the *costumbrista* (cos-toom-BRIS-tah) movement began. This genre was concerned with the portrayal of customs, manners, and lifestyles.

"Márquez has insights and sympathies which he can project with the intensity of a reflecting mirror in a bright sun."
—*New Statesman*

The best-known artist of the *costumbrista* era was Rámon Torres Méndez (1809—85), whose series of paintings entitled *Cuadros de Costumbres* (*Pictures of Customs*) was an almost complete visual guide to life at the end of the 19th century.

The *costumbrista* period was followed by one of great interest in realism and impressionism, inspired by the French movement.

Artists in the 20th century introduced progressive works following international trends. Alejandro Obregón (born in 1920) is considered by some critics to be the greatest living Colombian artist. Fernando Botero (born in 1932) is another world-renowned artist.

Other distinguished artists in Colombia include Judith Márquez Montoya, who has gained recognition with her many series of canvases on similar themes, and Ana Mercedes Hoyos (born in 1942), who has experimented with a "pop" style, with surrealism, and with exacting treatments of everyday objects.

ARCHITECTURE

Colombia's colonial architecture was consistent with Spanish styles and varied according to the climate in which it was being developed and according to the province from which the colonists originated. Fine colonial architecture can be seen in Santa Marta, Cartagena, Bogotá, Tunja, and Popayán.

Colombia has produced many internationally renowned pop stars. The most famous is Shakira (right). After the success of her album Barefoot *in 1995, Shakira began working with producer Emilio Estefan Jr. and recorded "Where Are the Thieves?," which sold millions worldwide. Shakira went on to make an English album called* Laundry Service, *which debuted at number three on the* Billboard *charts in the United States. Her most successful songs include "Hips Don't Lie," which sold more than 10 million copies worldwide, and her song, "She Wolf," released in October 2009. She is the winner of two American and seven Latin Grammys. In 2008 Shakira was nominated for a Golden Globe award. She is also a UNICEF Goodwill ambassador.*

Colombian singer—songwriter Juanes swept the Latin Grammys in 2003 with his album A Normal Day, *which has become very popular in the United States and Europe. He was chosen by CNN as a global icon, and his humanitarian activism has characterized him as the most supportive artist in the history of Spanish music.*

Ultramodern buildings are being constructed in the cities. In Bogotá wide boulevards with tall glass skyscrapers create a magnificent contrast to the impressive colonial quarter. Many modern Colombian architects have studied with leading architects in Europe and the United States, and architecture has become a very prestigious field. Works of particular merit include the Bank of Bogotá, Cartagena's baseball stadium, and the Luis Ángel Arango Library.

PERFORMING AND FOLK ARTS

Afro-Colombians and indigenous Colombians have had a strong influence on music in the coastal regions. Afro-Colombian rhythms such as fandangos, *porros* (POR-ros), and *maples* (MAH-plays) have also gained attention outside the country.

During his second term President Álvaro Uribe Vélez tried to cut funding to the cinema industry. He was heavily criticized for this and, in the end, funding was not cut.

DANCE Folk dance ranges from the Caribbean coast's exciting rhythmic steps to the *bambuco* (bam-BOO-ko), which resembles a waltz at a slightly quicker tempo. The *bambuco* is the national dance and is performed by couples. The salsa is a lively dance in which everyone whirls to trumpets and maracas. The *cumbia* (COOM-bee-ah) is an African-Colombian rhythm that has its listeners tapping their feet.

MUSIC Instruments typically used in Colombian music are the *flauta* (FLAO-tah), which is an Indian flute; the *tiple* (TEE-play), which is a many-stringed guitar-like instrument; and the *raspa* (RAHS-pah), which is made from a gourd and played like a washboard.

In the Popayán region, two types of traditional music prevail: the *murga* (MOOR-gah) and the *chirimía* (che-re-MEE-ah). The *murga* is performed by wandering bands of musicians playing *tiples*, *bandolas* (ban-DOH-las), guitars, mandolins, and accordions. *Chirimía* music is characteristic of the music of the indigenous people of the lower Andes. Although folk music is the dominant type of music, Colombians do also enjoy classical music. Bogotá is home to the National Symphony Orchestra and the National Conservatory, founded in 1882. Concerts and operas are held in Bogotá's Colón Theater.

The *cumbia* is a lively dance accompanied by African-Colombian music.

FILM AND DRAMA Colombia has a longstanding dramatic tradition. The country's first theater was established in the late 1700s. José Fernández Madrid (1789—1830) was considered the founder of the national theater, because he was the first Colombian dramatist to write about the New World. Enrique Buenaventura is a world-renowned Colombian playwright. He is the author of *A la derecha de Dios Padre* (*To the Right of God, the Father*), among others. He is also the founder of the Teatro Experimental de Cali (TEC).

Today Colombian drama is thriving, not only in the numerous theaters around the country but also on the silver screen. *Rodrigo D: No Future* (1990), directed by Victor Gaviria in a quasi-documentary style, was the first Colombian film to be showcased in the Cannes Film Festival.

In 2003 the Colombian government passed the Law of Cinema, which assisted local film production. Numerous films were sponsored by the government through taxes collected from distributors, exhibitors, and film producers. The local cinema industry started to get more vibrant with films such as *Soñar no cuesta nada* (*A Ton of Luck*) by Rodrigo Triana. It reached out to 1.2 million cinemagoers in Colombia alone, which was unprecedented.

INTERNET LINKS

www.buzzle.com/articles/culture-of-colombia.html
This site provides a concise overview of Colombia's art culture.

http://worldmusic.nationalgeographic.com/view/page.basic/country/content.country/colombia_48
This is an informative page on the various artists who define the Colombian music scene today. It includes pictures and links to websites belonging to the various groups.

www.onlinesalsa.com/news/world-s-top-salsa-dancing-from-colombia
This fascinating video shows authentic and very quick salsa dancing from Cali.

Close to a million people in Colombia earn a living directly or indirectly from the country's vibrant arts and crafts sector. A significant contributor to the national economy, the sector counts some 350,000 artisans. Approximately 60 percent of them are from rural and indigenous areas, and 65 percent of them are women.

LEISURE

Young men playing soccer on the waterfront in Cartagena.

11

COLOMBIA'S VARIED LANDSCAPE permits a great variety of outdoor activities. As in most Latin American countries, soccer is by far the favorite sport, though baseball and basketball have their share of devotees. The women's basketball league consists of teams representing the departments, or states, of the country. Colombian players also regularly participate in international table tennis competitions.

Colombians relaxing and catching up over a game of cards.

There is much greater access to recreational facilities in the cities than in the rural areas. In Bogotá, for example, there are countless opportunities for spectator and competitor alike, such as boxing tournaments in the Coliseo El Salitre and auto racing events. Golf, tennis, bowling, and skiing are also popular, but are generally affordable only for the wealthy.

WATER SPORTS

Water sports are quite popular among Colombians. They enjoy fishing for marlin, tarpon, dolphin, tuna, and sailfish any time of the year, and international fishing competitions are held in Barranquilla in the months of May and November.

The coast offers great opportunities for surfers. Swimming, water skiing, scuba-diving, and snorkeling are exciting diversions in the inlets and bays of the Pacific. The Rosario Islands off Cartagena are a favorite place for skin-diving, but only for the very daring—sharks and barracuda frequent these tempting, clear waters.

There are an estimated 300,000 to 400,000 trips made daily in Bogotá by bicycle.

Children playing with a mini foosball table at a childcare center in Boyaca.

MOUNTAINEERING

Scaling Colombia's mountains is a popular pastime, as are cycling and hiking. The Sierra Nevada, approximately 30 miles (48 km) from Santa Marta, provides one of the most exciting mountain-climbing experiences to be had anywhere in the world. The peaks of the Sierra Nevada are nearly 19,000 feet (5,791 m) high.

CYCLING

Professional cycling in Colombia became very popular after the triumphs of Martín Emilio "Cochise" Rodríguez in European cycling competitions, which in turn helped to develop the Colombian Cycling Federation. Rodríguez was later followed by a generation of bicyclers known as the Colombian beetles. These competitors created a fan base in Colombia, which helped create the *Vuelta de Colombia,* a local cycling competition.

During the 1990s the government of the Colombian capital, Bogotá, introduced bike paths, which became popular and were introduced later into other Colombian cities. The government of Bogotá later built Bogotá's Bike Paths Network to sponsor the practice of cycling by the population and to curve the city's increasing pollution by drivers. The network extends throughout the city and bicycle usage has increased fivefold in the city.

Cyclists along the road of Medellín. Like soccer, cycling is a popular sport in Colombia, and cycling races attract many participants and spectators.

The Copa America is a soccer competition among South American nations.

SOCCER

Soccer is the most popular sport in Colombia. Although it is not one of the leading soccer-playing nations in South America, Colombia has nonetheless produced some very outstanding teams at both the club and international level, as well as some talented individual players. The Colombian national soccer team participated in a FIFA World Cup tournament in 1962, 1990, 1994, and 1998. The best result was in 1990 when the team qualified for the second round of matches. Despite going into the quarterfinals of the Copa America 2011, the Colombian soccer team's best achievement to date was winning the Copa America 2001, which the country also hosted.

A matador avoiding the charging bull at a bullfight in Medellín. A bullfight pits the courage of the matador against the strength of the bull. This is why it is known as *la fiesta brava* (the brave festival).

HUNTING

Game hunting has long been a favorite sport among the wealthy. With tapirs, deer, and boar roaming the wilderness and organized safaris in the llanos of the Amazon basin, game hunters are never bored. Serious dove hunters have been visiting the Cauca Valley near Cali since 1975.

BULLFIGHTS

Bullfights are so popular that there are two bullfighters' unions, and most cities have *plazas de toros* (plah-sahs deh TOH-ros), or bullfighting rings. There are bullfights all year-round, but the most exciting ones are the international festivals in February and December, when visiting toreros, or bullfighters, arrive. Although bullfighting is a dangerous profession, it is a

COCKFIGHTS

Cockfights are popular among rural Colombians. Trained gamecocks are put beak to beak on a stage or in a pit and are let loose to fight one another. The gamecocks are usually fitted with razor-sharp spurs. The competition goes on until one of the cocks is either killed, can no longer fight, or refuses to fight.

There are three types of cockfights: the single battle, in which two roosters fight; the main battle, in which cocks are paired and play an elimination tournament; and the battle royal, in which several roosters fight one another until only one is left standing.

matter of grace, courage, and skill for the torero, the bullfighter who kills the bull. The bulls are bred specifically for fighting. They are aggressive, obstinate, and extremely strong.

Bullfights take place on Thursday and Sunday afternoons. In a typical program, three toreros fight two bulls each. Before the contest, they parade around the arena in their beautifully hand-tailored suits, called *trajes de luces* (TRAH-hays de LOO-ses), meaning "suits of lights." The toreros head the procession, armed with swords and followed by six-man teams, cuadrillas (kwa-DREE-lyas), with picadores to assist them. The crowds are screaming at fever-pitch by the time the parade is over, and then the bullfight begins. A trumpet sounds, the bullpen opens, and the bull charges out into the ring.

The picadores begin to taunt the bull so that the torero can observe its movements. He performs a few moves with the cape, called passes, without moving his feet. Then the picadores harass the bull by prodding its shoulders with lances, weakening its neck muscles. The banderilleros insert darts into the bull's upper back. Attached to the darts are ribbons, which are included for color.

Cockfighting is one of the many games on which Colombians like to bet.

TEJO

Tejo (TAY-ho) is a traditional game similar to horseshoes. Nearly every Colombian town has a tejo court. Two mounds of dirt are built around pipes that are set about 40 feet (12 m) apart. The tops of the pipes are leveled with the tops of the mounds of dirt and are loaded with small amounts of gunpowder, called mecha *(MAY-chah). The* tejo, *a smooth round piece of metal or stone, is thrown at the top of the mound, and the object of the game is to explode the* mecha.

There are tejo *experts throughout the countryside, and on Sundays after church or in the afternoons on market days, the sound of exploding* mechas *provides much excitement and commotion.*

For the third and final act, the torero first prepares the bull for the kill by means of a few graceful maneuvers. Well-executed passes draw cheers of "*Olé!*" from the crowd. After what the torero feels is the correct number of passes, he goes for the kill with a single swift thrust of the sword.

The most admired method of killing the bull is called the *recibiendo* (ray-see-be-EN-do). It is a perfectly executed thrust between the horns that kills the bull instantly. This maneuver is quite dangerous, because the torero must stand perfectly still while the enraged animal lunges toward him.

The more common procedure is the *volapié* (vo-lah-pe-AY), which allows the torero to dodge the charging bull and deliver the fatal blow between the shoulder blades. This is a dangerous sport, for a simple movement of the bull's horns can gore the torero. If the torero has performed successfully, the bull dies immediately and the crowd cheers. If not, the process is repeated with less enthusiasm from the crowd at each repetition.

BETTING

An activity that is very popular between both rich and poor is gambling on games of chance. Estimates indicate that Colombians spend as much as 25 percent of their regular income on gambling, regardless of how small or large that income is.

Lotteries are prevalent throughout the country. They are thought to serve an important social function, because the country's welfare program and hospitals receive a generous portion of the profits.

In addition to this government-sponsored activity, there are numerous gambling casinos and horseracing tracks, and there is always considerable wagering on other sporting events, such as soccer, bullfights, and cockfights.

SPORTS IN RURAL AREAS

In rural areas there are sports clubs and leagues affiliated with the local churches or sponsored by municipalities. Chess, bicycle races, soccer, volleyball, and *tejo* are the activities most likely to occupy the residents of the countryside in their leisure time.

INTERNET LINKS

www.lonelyplanet.com/colombia/travel-tips-and-articles/12948

This fascinating page explains *tejo*, the national sport of Colombia, with useful pictures.

www.cas-international.org/en/home/suffering-of-bulls-and-horses/bullfighting/colombia/

This site includes vivid descriptions of bullfighting in Colombia.

http://vimeo.com/7775135

This is a beautiful video on cycling through the Andes Mountains in Colombia.

Colombia's bullfighting season runs from mid-January to the end of February every year. However, this sport or art form is facing increasing criticism as cruelty to animals. There are five countries in Latin America that have bullfighting, and Colombia is now the Latin American country with the most anti-bullfighting municipalities.

FESTIVALS

The word *carnival* evokes a vision of glittering costumes and unending merrymaking, but Colombian carnivals are more subdued than those in other parts of South America. Still, there is much dancing in the street.

12

T HE WORD *FIESTA* BRINGS TO MIND a whimsical celebration with laughter, dancing, music, and merriment. There may be much ringing of church bells and even fireworks. However, there is usually a serious reason behind the activities, and often a somber tone pervades the celebration of these special events.

Colombia is a land of festivals and fairs, as the nation holds several hundred fairs and festivals a year.

Locals dressed as animals at the Carnival of Barranquilla—a festival of colors on the Caribbean coast of Colombia.

"The Dance of the Devils" at the annual Corpus Christi festival. Held in Indian territory, this Christian religious event usually coincides with the summer solstice celebrated by black African slaves. As a result of the confluence, Indian myths, the African animistic rites, and other pre-Columbian features have blended with the Spanish Catholic festival into a lively spectacle.

FIESTAS

Fiestas in Colombia are held to commemorate milestones in the life of the nation or of its communities. Fiestas of indigenous groups may mark the harvest, a child's first haircut, or seasonal changes, such as the beginning of the rainy season. Civic festivities usually include speeches, parades, and sometimes athletic competitions.

Religious fiestas are usually the most numerous and most colorful. Although there is a serious and solemn background to each feast day, the purpose behind the celebration is both religious and entertaining. Generally a rural fiesta will emphasize the worship aspect. Special Masses mark the day as well as a procession that features a holy image and great ceremony. Often a market day will be coordinated with the activities, so vendors can display their wares for a large crowd.

FERIAS

Fiestas that are associated with a religious pilgrimage and that last a week or more are called ferias. Dancing is usually part of the religious ferias. Two kinds of dance are usually performed at ferias: ritual and folk dances.

SAN ISIDRO

April marks the end of the dry season in Colombia. On April 4 the image of San Isidro (Saint Isadore the Farmer), who is responsible for bringing the rains, is carried through the town of Río Frío. All the townspeople follow his image and chant his praises.

In their chanting, the local farmers explain the need for rain, and optimally, San Isidro will cooperate by bringing the first shower before the celebration is completed. So as not to demand too much of the saint, the parade is slow and drawn out. For every two steps the participants take, they take one step back!

If San Isidro has not cooperated after several processions through the town, the tone of the chanting changes from praise to scolding. As the hours pass, the yelling becomes progressively more belligerent until the townspeople can be heard screaming profanities! Should there be no change in the skies, San Isidro is put away until the next April, when the worshipers will hope for better results.

Ritual dances take place in the courtyard or main grounds of the church. Women generally do not take part in them. A ritual dance is considered a serious matter and usually includes a dramatization and dialogue for a specific purpose, such as honoring a saint. Alternatively a folk dance is a social matter. Its main purpose is to entertain, and it can be performed by men and women of all ages.

Some of the most colorful festivals are those of the indigenous groups and Afro-Caribbeans. Among the Andean groups, as a result of missionary efforts, there has been a blending of Christian saints and pagan gods. For example many indigenous people do not see much difference between the *Mama* (Mother Nature) and the Virgin Mary. Coastal Afro-Colombians have combined their traditional rituals and beliefs with those of Christianity.

Regardless of whether the celebration is strictly Christian, an Indian ritual, or a hodgepodge of African, Christian, and pagan ceremonies, the fiesta is an opportunity to bring zest and color into lives that are often a simple and trying struggle. The festival is a wonderful contrast to the everyday routine of labor and poverty. Because it occurs yearly, it is a magical time for all to anticipate. It becomes a project for all in the community to plan and revel in when spirited times begin.

The origins of the Festival of Blacks and Whites date back to times of the Spanish rule when slaves were allowed to celebrate on January 5 and their masters showed their approval on January 6 by painting their faces black. On these days the slaves either put grease or talcum powder on their faces.

DÍA DE NEGRITOS/FIESTA DE LOS BLANQUITOS (CARNIVAL OF BLACKS AND WHITES)

In Popayán during the first week of January, there is a Mardi Gras atmosphere to celebrate the end of the Christmas season. January 5 is the *Día de Negritos* (Day of the Black Ones), and the next day is the *Fiesta de los Blanquitos* (Festival of the White Ones). Many people think that the color references are to the biblical Three Wise Men, who reached their destination on the sixth day of the month. However, the days actually get their names from the activities that take place on those days.

On the morning of the Día de Negritos, boys with shoe polish chase the girls of the community and decorate them with their blackened hands. As the day progresses, older boys chase after older girls, and by the time evening falls, no one is safe from the marauding boys.

The frivolity of present-day celebrations of the Día de Negritos derives from more dignified practices in olden days, when gentlemen would parade beneath balconies until the ladies came to the door. The men were then allowed to paint a spot on the ladies' cheek or forehead. The festivities have grown more rowdy over the years, and today many people prefer to stay indoors to avoid the fracas.

There are still street parades in the afternoon with people in masquerade and *chirimias*, or strolling groups, playing the latest Colombian *bambucos* on traditional instruments. At the main square, the *tasajo* (tay-SAH-ho), or distribution of foods donated by rich farm owners, takes place. When night falls the celebrations continue at a social club or in private homes, with dancing and partying until dawn.

The following morning, white becomes the focus of the celebration. Boys chase girls in the streets with white flour and ride around town tossing the flour on everyone they see. People on balconies pour water on the flour-coated pedestrians, until everyone is laden with a sticky mixture. There is much merrymaking and drinking. Older Colombians may recall how the day was once marked by beautiful religious celebrations.

CARNIVAL

Colombians wearing colorful ribbon hats at a festival.

The word *carnival* comes from the Latin phrase *carne vale* (farewell to flesh), which aptly describes the fasting of Lent in the days leading up to Easter. The philosophy behind the carousing is that indulgence in one's desires before the fast will make it easier to realize the oncoming religious experience. The whole country participates in the festivities of Carnival. However, the celebration in Barranquilla is most elaborate. The city begins preparing for Carnival just after Christmas, and the two months preceding Lent are filled with masquerades and dancing in the public square.

Several ritual dances are performed during Carnival: The *maestranza* is a comical dance performed by men dressed as women; the *danza de los pájaros* (DAHN-sah de los PAH-ha-ros) is also danced by men wearing colorful costumes, including plumage and masks with beaks.

The festival of Colombia's patron saint, the Virgin Mary of the Rosary of Chinquinquirá, is one of the most famous in the Americas.

CALENDAR OF FESTIVALS

January	1	New Year's Day
	6	Epiphany Day (Three Kings Day)
February	2	Candlemas
March	19	Saint Joseph's Day
March/April		Maundy Thursday
		Good Friday
		Holy Saturday
		Easter Sunday
May	1	Labor Day
		Ascension Day
June		Corpus Christi
	29	Saints Peter and Paul Day
July	20	Independence Day
August	7	Battle of Boyacá
	15	Feast of the Assumption
October	12	Columbus Day
November	1	All Saints' Day
	11	Independence of Cartagena
December	8	Feast of the Immaculate Conception
	25	Christmas

The *coyongo* (co-YON-go) is a ritual dance-drama. A coyongo is a large aquatic fishing bird. In this dance several "birdmen" circle a man dressed as a fish, who tries to evade the "birdmen" as they close in on him.

INDEPENDENCE OF CARTAGENA

This annual carnival takes place on the November 11, the anniversary of the Declaration of Independence of Cartagena. The old walled city holds a four-day celebration featuring thousands of costumed people dancing in the streets to the sound of maracas and drums. There are parades, floral displays, and frenzied excitement caused by fireworks called *buscapiés* (boos-cah-PYESS), or feet searchers that send crowds reeling as the firecrackers bounce along the streets.

People dance throughout the night and wander in the streets to the music of guitars, maracas, and drums. The festivities culminate with the National Beauty Contest's selection of the young woman who will represent Colombia in international beauty contests.

The Cali Fair is held in Cali from December 25 to New Year's Eve. It is famous for its salsa marathon concerts attended by renowned salsa bands. There are horse-riding parades, masquerades, and dances.

INTERNET LINKS

www.escapefromamerica.com/2011/02/festival-in-bogota-colombia/
This is a comprehensive guide to festivals in Colombia.

www.gowealthy.com/gowealthy/wcms/en/home/articles/entertainment/events-and-festivals/Festivals-in-Colombia-f2jwkm2roW.html
This site provides a concise guide to the most important festivals in Colombia.

www.colombia.travel/en/international-tourist/sightseeing-what-to-do/history-and-tradition/fairs-and-festivals
This is the official guide to festivals in Colombia, complete with a zesty picture slideshow at the bottom of the page.

FOOD

Locals enjoying a cup of coffee at a shop in Colombia.

13

COLOMBIAN FOOD generally uses a lot of potatoes and rice, and stews and soups also feature prominently on the Colombian menu, which is not excessively spicy. Poultry is the preferred meat. In recent years meat consumption in the country has shifted away from beef, because poultry can be bought at lower prices and is considered a healthier meat alternative.

Colombian cuisine is very diverse and varies from region to region.

Fresh fruit is available in abundance at the daily market.

Coffee is the national drink, found in almost every Colombian household. According to a survey conducted in 1999, nearly 90 percent of all households in Colombia served coffee at least once a day.

The Colombian kitchen is simply the room in which meals are prepared. The family does not eat in the kitchen; they eat in the dining room instead. Colombian homes do not have dine-in kitchens or breakfast nooks like those that are common in the United States. Nearly all rural homes in Colombia now have electrical power and a running water supply. However, rural kitchens may not be equipped with the electrical appliances used in urban homes, such as microwave ovens.

Colombians have a strong cultural bias against standing water. As a result they prefer not to leave dirty plates to soak in the sink. Instead they wash their dishes immediately under running water. Maids seldom close the drain in the sink or collect water in a dishpan to clean up after a meal. Rather they keep the water running, scrape everything off the dish, and then wash it with a soapy sponge before rinsing it under the running faucet.

A Colombian family preparing a meal in a spacious Colombian kitchen.

For breakfast, people in Bogotá often eat *changua*—a soup made from milk, scallions, and eggs.

As a result dishes are washed in cold water. It is customary to leave the water running for long periods of time. It also makes perfect sense not to soak the dishes, because dirty dishes bathed in cold water would certainly lead to an unsavory mess!

Hot water heaters are also not common in Colombia. In rural areas water for cooking, bathing, and washing clothes is boiled in a large pot over the fire or gas stove. City dwellers have water heaters that must be lit. Because gas is expensive, some families have their maid light the water heater each morning so that there is sufficient water for the family to shower, and it is routinely turned off after breakfast.

THE NATIONAL DRINK

There are four types of Colombian coffee: caturra *(kah-TOO-rah),* maragojipe *(mah-rah-goh-HEE-pay),* pajarito *(pah-hah-REE-to), and* borbón *(bor-BON). Coffee plants are grown under banana trees, which shade them from direct sunlight. Because only the ripest beans can be harvested, they must be hand-picked and dried on racks for several days. In some villages it is the job of the children to turn the beans so that both sides are thoroughly dried.*

Supremo (so-PRAY-mo) is the highest grade of beans; extra (EX-trah) is a lower grade. Excelso (ex-SAHL-so) is a blend of the high- and lower-grade beans. This blend of coffee is exported to the United States in larger quantities than any other coffee.

In Colombia meals are often served with coffee. A small cup of black coffee is called a tinto, *and it often contains a lot of sugar. Coffee with milk is known as* café perico *(kah-FAY pay-REE-co);* café con leche *(kah-FAY con LAY-chay) is warm milk with coffee.*

There are no coffee breaks in Colombian offices because people drink coffee around the clock. In fact a person may travel from desk to desk and dispense tintos. *Typical Colombians between the ages of 12 and 64 consume at least one cup of coffee a day.*

FOOD SHOPPING

A wide range of food and household items is available at the supermarkets in the main cities.

Shopping in Colombia's major cities is very similar to shopping in the United States. Colombia has one of the most modern supermarket sectors in Latin America. The large supermarket chains are Cafam, Carulla, Fortuna, Ley, and Olímpica, and there are also hypermarkets, such as Carrefour. Almost any item can be found in the city, but many foods are imported and are only available in delicatessens and specialty stores.

A wide variety of fruit and vegetables is available throughout the year. They are usually moderately priced, but fruit imported from the United States, such as pears, apples, and plums, can be costly. Meats are a bit less expensive than they are in the United States. Yet they are usually leaner—because the animals are grass-fed—and they taste somewhat different because they are fresh. In small towns or in the neighborhood meat market, there may be no refrigeration. When pork or beef arrives from the slaughterhouse, a red flag is hung out so that customers know the meat has arrived. They buy up the meat quickly and take it home to prepare the next meal.

Rural villages usually have a small store, or *tienda* (tee-AYN-dah), where people buy food, beer, and other items. The *tienda* is also a social center, where villagers come to visit and share gossip. A *tienda* may be no more than a room, perhaps attached to the owner's house, with a counter where employees gather merchandise for customers.

Most Colombian towns and villages have more than one *tienda*, and these *tiendas* are open every day of the week. The *tienda* competes with the modern convenience store and the large supermarket by offering its wide middle- and lower-income consumer base advantages such as proximity and credit.

MEALTIMES

Breakfast, lunch, and dinner are traditional mealtimes in Colombia. Breakfast is not a family meal, and everyone eats according to the needs of his or her personal schedule. The father, who may have to leave for work as early as 7:00 A.M., will eat breakfast earliest. The children's breakfast time depends on whether they have to go to school and what time the school bus picks them up. Breakfast foods vary by region, but usually include eggs, soup, bread, fruit, juice, and, of course, Colombian coffee to perk the adults up.

Lunch, on the other hand, is the most important meal for the family, and the father returns home for it. This may be his only opportunity to spend time with his children because he may not return home in the evening before their bedtime. Lunch is eaten at around 12:30 or 1:00 P.M. and may last until 2:30 P.M. Soup, rice, meat with vegetables, and dessert are the typical courses for the midday meal.

The evening meal, eaten at around 7:00 or 8:00 P.M, may include soup, rice, meat, potatoes, salad, and beans.

Colombians typically eat three meals a day: breakfast, a large lunch between 12:00 and 2:00 P.M., and a light dinner.

A typical lunch consisting of ground beef, corn and mushrooms in Colombia.

A Colombian family enjoying their meal. On market days, food stalls sell a variety of local dishes.

TABLE MANNERS

Table manners in the Colombian home are similar to those in homes in the United States. One practice that is different, however, is that Colombians feel that the left hand should be kept visible above the table.

Colombians are quite formal at mealtimes. Wearing pajamas or a bathrobe and slippers to breakfast is not acceptable. At lunch and dinner, everyone in the family is expected to dress as though they were ready to dine out. Pleasant conversation is always welcome during meals, and it is considered impolite to eat too much or to take food without first offering it to others. If the host offers more refreshments, the guest politely declines. When a person has finished eating, he or she places the silverware horizontally across the plate.

FOODS OF COLOMBIA

Colombian foods are rich and heavily seasoned, but not necessarily spicy. Starches are a large part of the Colombian diet, including potatoes, rice, and a root called yucca. Generally the Colombian menu is a mixture of Indian and Spanish traditions. What individuals select from a menu reflects economic status and regional tastes.

A dish that is popular throughout the country is *ajiaco* (ah-hee-AH-coh), a highly seasoned soup of potatoes, chicken, capers, corn, and slices of avocado. Soup is served much more often and in many more varieties in Colombia than

HIGH-ALTITUDE COOKING

In Medellín, Bogotá, and other regions above 5,000 feet (1,524 m), people practice high-altitude cooking. Because air has less pressure at higher altitudes, recipes must be modified to preserve the quality of the food being cooked.

Foods that suffer most from changes in altitude are those that require baking or boiling and those that contain a lot of sugar. Water boils at a higher temperature at higher altitudes, so it takes a longer time to prepare boiled foods. Pressure cookers are quite helpful in such cases.

Because most breads and cakes depend on yeast or baking powder for their shape and consistency, the decreased pressure makes it necessary to reduce the leavening agents so cakes and breads do not collapse. For baking in the highlands, the rule of thumb is to reduce baking powder, shortening, and sugar slightly and increase eggs and liquid slightly.

in the United States. It is even occasionally served as breakfast or as a main course. *Changua* (CHAN-guh-ah) soup is a favorite Andean breakfast. It is a blend of beef broth, milk, and chopped coriander.

Sopa de pan (SO-pah de PAHN) is a main course soup that uses bread, eggs, and cheese. It is quite filling and full of nutrients. Other popular soups are made with vegetables, plantains (a fruit similar to the banana), rice, and potatoes.

Some very tasty breads are served in Colombia. *Arepa* (ah-RAY-pah) is a simple cornroll of Indian origin. It is made of ground corn mixed with a little salt and enough water to make a stiff dough, which is then toasted on a greased griddle. *Arepa* is eaten by rich and poor alike. *Mogollos* (mo-GOL-lyos) are whole-wheat muffins with a raisin-flavored center that are served with dinner. *Roscones* (ros-KO-nes) are buns filled with guava jelly and sprinkled with sugar.

The *arepa* is a tasty cornbread enjoyed by all Colombians.

Because cattle are pasture fed, Colombian beef is somewhat tougher than beef from the United States, but Colombian cooks have found some wonderfully tasty ways to tenderize and prepare it. Rather than grinding the beef into hamburger meat, they slice it into tiny cubes. The meat is sautéed, broiled, or added to soups. The small size of the cubes prevents the meat from becoming too tough. Another zesty Colombian tenderizing method is to simmer a chunk of meat for several hours and then baste and roast it for several more hours.

REGIONAL DELICACIES

Regional favorites have much to do with the types of vegetables and fruit that grow in the area. For example the high, cool mountain valleys near Bogotá produce white potatoes in abundance, and the recipes of that region make good use of this vegetable. *Papas chorreadas* (PAH-pas chor-ray-AH-das) are boiled potatoes covered with a flavorful sauce of coriander, cream, tomatoes, cheese, and scallions.

Beef is the most plentiful meat in Colombia, and in rural areas, it is broiled over a charcoal fire by the roadside.

PAPAS CHORREADAS

2 tablespoons (30 ml) butter

1 teaspoon (5 ml) coriander

4 scallions

pinch of dried oregano

½ cup (125 ml) finely chopped onions

pinch of cumin

5 medium tomatoes, peeled, seeded, and chopped

½ teaspoon (2.5 ml) salt

1 cup (250 ml) grated mozzarella cheese

½ cup (125 ml) heavy cream

8 large potatoes, peeled, and boiled

Heat butter over moderate heat in a 10-inch (25.4-cm) skillet. Add scallions and onions and stir frequently for 5 minutes or until the onions are soft and transparent. Add tomatoes and cook, stirring for 5 minutes. Add cream, coriander, oregano, cumin, and salt, stirring constantly. Continue stirring and add cheese. Stir until cheese melts. Serve over sliced boiled potatoes.

Although the region around Bogotá is cool, the warm zones are quite close by, and the cooks of the capital city have an abundance of tropical fruit available to them. Bananas and avocados are favorite ingredients. There are perhaps a dozen ways that the people of Bogotá prepare green bananas. Avocados are added to all types of salads and soups.

People of Indian and African descent who inhabit the jungles grow yucca, corn, beans, and plantains, and they catch local wildlife for meat. They eat monkeys, tapirs, and any kind of bird, except parrot, whose flesh is too tough. Ants are a delicacy among Colombian villagers and jungle dwellers. The insects are caught in large quantities during mating season and are fried in oil or fat.

In the western part of the country, particularly the Cauca valley, there is a distinctive local cuisine that makes wonderful use of the yucca and plantain that thrive in the warm climate. The leathery leaves of the plantain are used to wrap various mixtures of corn and other ingredients for steaming and boiling. One such treat is *hallaca* (al-YAH-kah), which is similar to the tamales of Mexico.

DINING OUT

There is an exciting variety of international restaurants in larger cities, especially in Bogotá, where there are restaurants that serve Swiss, Middle Eastern, and other cuisines.

However, many Colombian restaurants take pride in serving dishes typical of their region. At finer restaurants waiters are particularly polite and provide excellent service. There may be as many as three to four waiters per table to meet the diners' every need.

Fast-food lovers can find some of their favorites in Bogotá. Burger King and Pizza Hut outlets dot the city streets, although the food there can be expensive. There are also local hamburger shops in all the major cities, and cantinas sell snacks, tropical fruit juices, and coffee. Bogotá also has many bars, cafés, and nightclubs for after-dinner entertainment.

The Colombian *hallaca* makes use of plantain leaves to wrap the ingredients instead of the cornhusk favored in Mexico.

DRINKING CUSTOMS

Colombians do not drink much at meals. Coffee, however, being the national beverage, is often consumed with meals. Children usually drink milk with their meals. Fruit juices and colas are favorite soft drinks, and they are usually highly sweetened because Colombians love sugar.

The hosts of a party always encourage their guests to have an alcoholic beverage, and declining an invitation to "join the party" would be regarded as snobbish behavior.

Beer is a favorite drink between meals, and in rural areas it is occasionally taken with meals. Wine is served at dinner, when there are guests, but it is not typically served at family meals. Colombia produces very little wine, and imported wines can be very expensive.

A traditional Indian alcoholic beverage is a potent corn liquor called *chicha* (CHEE-chah). Although the government outlawed chicha in 1948, the drink's popularity has not suffered, especially in rural areas, where alcohol is an important part of community life on market days, on visits to the *tienda*, and on other occasions.

Other favorite Colombian liquors are rum, a fermented brown sugar called *guarapo* (gwa-RAH-po), and a licorice-flavored liquor called *aguardiente* (ah-goo-ahr-dee-AYN-tay). Every department produces its own brand of *aguardiente*, a great source of pride for the residents.

The *tienda* is a small grocery store and convenient meeting place for villagers.

Aguardiente (literally meaning "burning water") is an alcoholic drink derived from sugarcane. It is widely consumed at Colombian parties, and ranges in potency from 20 percent to 40 percent alcohol.

INTERNET LINKS

www.southamerica.cl/Colombia/Food.htm

This site provides a comprehensive overview of typical Colombian foods and how they are presented.

www.mycolombianrecipes.com/

This is an exquisite food recipe blog by a Colombian woman who is married to an American. It includes mouth-watering pictures.

http://seecolombia.travel/blog/2011/06/anthony-bourdain-no-reservations-in-colombia/

This excellent video with celebrity chef Anthony Bourdain explores the culinary delights of Cartagena, Colombia.

AJIACO DE POLLO BOGOTANO (BOGOTÁ CHICKEN SOUP)

This recipe makes six servings.

2 ounces (55 g) butter

3 pounds (1.5 kg) chicken, serving
  size pieces

2 finely chopped large onions

8 thinly sliced medium potatoes

2½ pints (1.5 L) chicken stock

6 new, or small red, potatoes

2 ears of corn, each cut into 3 pieces

3 tablespoons (45 ml) capers

1 pint (0.6 L) heavy cream

Salt and pepper

Cumin seeds (optional)

Heat butter in a heavy casserole dish, and sauté chicken pieces with onion until the chicken is golden. Add thinly sliced potatoes and chicken stock. Cover and cook over low heat for about 25 minutes. Add new potatoes and cook for about 20 minutes or until the chicken and potatoes are tender. Remove chicken pieces and potatoes, and work the stock through a sieve. Return stock to the casserole, and season with cumin, salt, and pepper to taste. Add chicken and potatoes, corn, and capers. Simmer for 5 minutes. Add cream and simmer just long enough to heat through. Serve in deep soup plates.

EMPANADAS (FILLED PASTRY)

This recipe makes six servings.

¼ cup (60 ml) raisins

1 tablespoon (14.8 ml) apple cider vinegar

1 pound (0.5 kg) ground beef or turkey

1 small chopped onion

2 cloves finely chopped garlic

1¾ cups (435 ml) salsa

¼ cup (60 ml) slivered almonds

2 tablespoons (30 ml) brown sugar

½ teaspoon (2.5 ml) ground cinnamon

pinch of salt

½ cup (125 ml) shredded cheddar cheese

1 pound (450 g) frozen bread dough, thawed

1 lightly beaten egg

Preheat the oven to 375°F (191°C). Combine raisins and vinegar in a small bowl. Soak for 15 to 20 minutes or until raisins are plump. Cook meat (beef or turkey), onion, and garlic in a large skillet until meat is browned. Drain. Add ½ cup (118 ml) salsa, almonds, raisins, sugar, cinnamon, and salt. Bring to a boil. Cook for 3 to 4 minutes or until flavors are blended. Divide dough into six pieces and roll into balls. On a well-floured board, roll each ball into a 6-inch (15.2-cm) circle. Place ½ cup (118 ml) meat filling on the bottom half of the circle. Sprinkle with cheese. Fold top half of the dough over the filling. Crimp edges with tines of a fork. Pierce top with the fork. Place on a greased cookie sheet. Brush with egg. Bake for 20 to 25 minutes or until golden. Serve with remaining salsa.

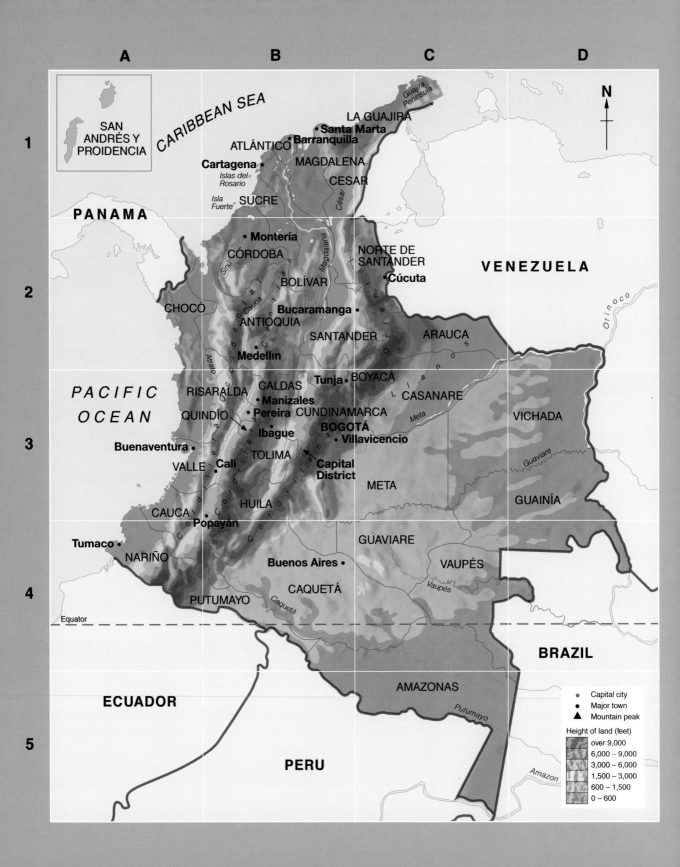

MAP OF COLOMBIA

Amazonas state,
  B4—B5, C4—C5,
  D4—D5
Amazon River,
  C5, D5
Antioquia state,
  A2, B2—B3
Arauca state, C2,
  D2
Atlántico state, B1
Atrato River, A2,
  B2—B3

Barranquilla, B1
Bogotá, B3
Bolívar state,
  B1—B2
Boyacá, B2—B3,
  C2—C3
Brazil, C4—C5,
  D4—D5
Bucaramanga, C2
Buenos Aires, B4

Caldas state, B3
Cali, B3
Caquetá River, B4,
  C4—C5, D5
Caquetá state,
  B3—B4, C4
Caribbean Sea,
  A1—A2, B1—B2
Cartagena, B1
Casanare, C2—C3
Cauca River, B2—B3
Cauca state,
  A3— A4, B3—B4

César River, B1—B2
César state, B1—B2,
  C1—C2
Chocó state,
  A2—A3, B2—B3
Cordillera Central,
  B2—B3
Cordillera
  Occidental,
  A3—A4, B2—B3
Cordillera Oriental,
  B3—B4, C2—C3
Córdoba, B1—B2
Cúcuta, C2
Cundinamarca, B3

Ecuador, A4—A5,
  B4—B5
Equator, A4, B4, C4,
  D4

Guainía state, C3—
  C4, D3—D4
Guajira Peninsula, C1
Guaviare River, B4,
  C3, D3
Guaviare State, B4,
  C3—C4

Huila state, B3—B4

Ibagué, B3
Isla Fuerte, B1
Islas del Rosario, B1

La Guajira state, C1
Llanos, C2—C3

Magdalena River,
  B1—B2
Magdalena state,
  B1—B2
Manizales, B3
Medellín, B2
Meta River, C2
Meta state,
  B3—B4, C3
Montería, B2

Nariño state,
  A3—A4
Norte de Santander
  state, B2, C2

Orinoco River,
  D2—D3

Pacific Ocean,
  A2—A4
Panama, A1—A2
Pereira, B3
Peru, A5, B4—B5,
  C5
Popayán, B3

Putumayo River,
  C5, D5
Putumayo state,
  A4, B4

Quindío state, B3

Risaralda state,
  B2—B3

San Andrés y
  Providencia, A1
Santa Marta, B1
Santander state,
  B2—B3, C2—C3
Sinú River, B1—B2
Sucre state, B1—B2

Tumaco, A4
Tunja, B3

Valle state, A3, B3
Vaupés River, C4
Vaupés state, C4
Venezuela, C1—C2,
  D1—D2
Villavicencio, B3

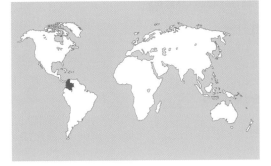

133

ECONOMIC COLOMBIA

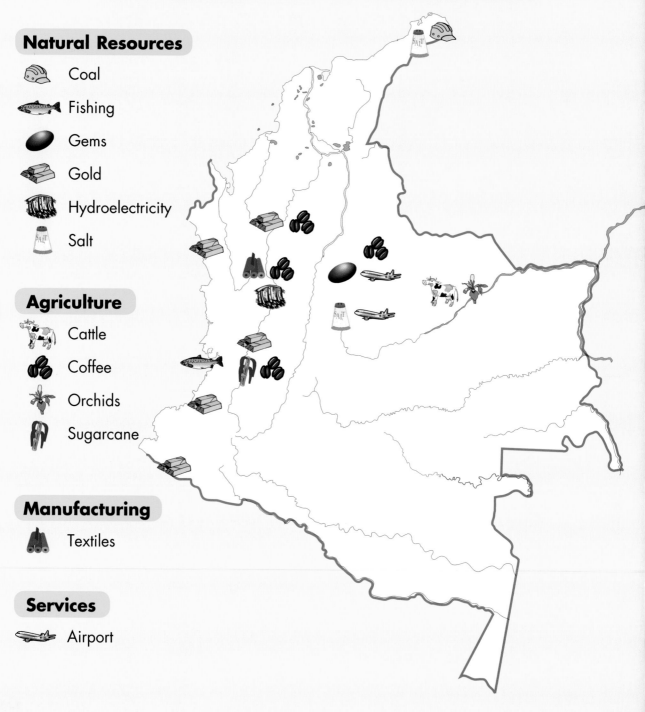

Natural Resources
- Coal
- Fishing
- Gems
- Gold
- Hydroelectricity
- Salt

Agriculture
- Cattle
- Coffee
- Orchids
- Sugarcane

Manufacturing
- Textiles

Services
- Airport

ABOUT THE ECONOMY

OVERVIEW

President Santos has introduced legislation to compensate Colombians who lost their land due to decades of violence. He also seeks to build on improvements in domestic security and on President Uribe's pro-business economic policies. Pro-business reforms in the oil and gas sectors and export-led growth, fueled mainly by the Andean Trade Promotion and Drug Eradication Act, have enhanced Colombia's investment climate. But inequality, underemployment, and drug trafficking remain significant challenges, and Colombia's infrastructure requires major improvements to sustain economic expansion. Colombia is a modest exporter of oil.

GROSS DOMESTIC PRODUCT (GDP)

$431.9 billion (2010 estimate)
Agriculture 9.3 percent, industry 38 percent, and services 52.7 percent

TERRITORY

Land: 401,044 square miles (1,038,700 square km)
Water: 38,691 square miles (100,210 square km)
Total: 439,736 square miles (1,138,910 square km)

CURRENCY

Peso (1 peso = 100 centavos)
$1 = 1,900 pesos (2011 estimate)

AGRICULTURAL PRODUCTS

Coffee, freshly cut flowers, bananas, sugarcane, cotton, rice, tobacco, corn, oilseed, vegetables, forest products, shrimp.

LABOR FORCE

21.27 million (2010 estimate)

UNEMPLOYMENT RATE

11.8 percent (2010 estimate)

INFLATION RATE

3.1 percent (2010 estimate)

MAIN EXPORTS

Petroleum, coffee, coal, nickel, emeralds, apparel, bananas, cut flowers

MAIN IMPORTS

Industrial and transportation equipment, consumer goods, chemicals, electricity, fuels, paper products

MAJOR TRADING PARTNERS

United States, China, European Union, Mexico, Brazil, Ecuador

PORTS AND HARBORS

Bahía de Portete, Barranquilla, Buenaventura, Cartagena, Leticia, Puerto Bolivar, San Andrés, Santa Marta, Tumaco, and Turbo

TELECOMMUNICATIONS

Land lines: 7.2 million
Mobile cellular: 43 million
Internet: 48.7 percent (2010 estimate)

MOTOR VEHICLES

67 per 1,000 inhabitants

CULTURAL COLOMBIA

El Laguito and Bocagrande
Cartagena's main tourist centers boast beaches lined with large hotels, restaurants, cafés, and fruit and ice-cream stalls. There are opportunities for all kinds of water sports. Underwater reserves near Cartagena make this an ideal place for diving.

Seafood Paradise
Numerous restaurants on the coast offer fresh seafood prepared in a variety of ways. Diners can feast on local seafood delicacies in the historical ambience of rebuilt ships and forts.

La Macarena Bull Ring
The bullfighting season is between January and February. The most important bullfights take place in February and December, when top matadors from Colombia and other countries meet for the international festival.

La Érmita
Cali's landmark, built in 1678 and renovated in 1930 after an earthquake, was inspired by Gothic architectural styles and has altars built by an Italian sculptor.

Día de Negritos and Fiesta de los Blanquitos
Every January 5, Popayán residents paint their faces with shoe polish to celebrate the Day of the Blacks. The next day, the Day of the Whites, everyone throws flour on one another.

San Agustín
Stone carvings and figures left by ancient Indian communities have made this village one of the most important archaeological sites in Colombia. The main collection of statues is in the archaeological park, almost 2 miles (3.2 km) from the village.

Music and theater
Bogotá is the home of the National Symphony Orchestra of Colombia and also big theater groups such as the Teatro Popular de Bogotá and Teatro Nacional.

Santa Marta
White sandy beaches and a calm sea make the area around Santa Marta a good place for water sports. Taganga, a nearby fishing village, offers snorkeling and diving opportunities.

Carnival
Hundreds of dancers and musicians dressed in elaborate costumes lead the crowds in feverish dancing all night in this celebration of indulgences before the 40-day Lenten fast.

Cathedral of Zipaquirá
This unique cathedral was carved by miners inside a huge salt mine in Zipaquirá, two hours north of Bogotá. The ceiling rises 75 feet (23 m) high over the altar, a block of salt weighing 19 tons (18 metric tons).

Museo del Oro
About 30,000 pieces of pre-Columbian art provide glimpses of ancient Indian spirituality. Flasks called *poporo*, for example, held the lime that tribal priests used to extract cocaine from the leaves they chewed to communicate with the spirits.

OFFICIAL NAME

República de Colombia (Republic of Colombia)

CAPITAL

Santa Fe de Bogotá

DEPARTMENTS (STATES)

Amazonas, Antioquia, Arauca, Atlántico, Bolívar, Boyacá, Caldas, Caquetá, Casanare, Cauca, César, Chocó, Córdoba, Cundinamarca, Guainía, Guaviare, Huila, La Guajira, Magdalena, Meta, Nariño, Norte de Santander, Putumayo, Quindío, Risaralda, San Andrés y Providencia, Santander, Sucre, Tolima, Valle del Cauca, Vaupés, Vichada, Bogotá Capital District

DESCRIPTION OF FLAG

Three horizontal stripes: yellow stands for Colombia, blue for the ocean separating Colombia from Spain, and red for the blood shed for freedom from Spain

POPULATION

44,725,543 (2011 estimate)

LIFE EXPECTANCY

Male: 71.27 years
Female: 78.03 years (2011 estimate)

ETHNIC GROUPS

Mixed Spanish and indigenous 58 percent, Caucasian 20 percent, mixed African and Caucasian 14 percent, African 4 percent, mixed indigenous and African 3 percent, and indigenous 1 percent

MAJOR LANGUAGES

Spanish is the official language. Some Indian groups speak their own languages. The San Andrés and Providencia Islanders speak English.

MAJOR RELIGIONS

Roman Catholicism 80 percent, different forms of Christianity 13.5 percent, other faiths 4.5 percent, agnostic 2 percent

GOVERNMENT SYSTEM

A constitutional republic with bicameral Congress, with a 102-seat Senate and 161-seat Chamber of Representatives. Separation of powers among the executive, judicial, and legislative branches

LEADERS IN POLITICS

Simón Bolívar (1763—1830)—liberator of the Spanish colonies and first president of Gran Colombia; Francisco de Paula Santander (1792—1840)—Bolívar's right-hand man during the struggle for independence and first elected president of Colombia; Álvaro Uribe Vélez—president from August 7, 2002, to August 7, 2010; Juan Manuel Santos Calderón—president from August 7, 2010 to present

TIME LINE

IN COLOMBIA	IN THE WORLD

A.D. 200s
The Chibchas farm, mine salt and emeralds, and trade with other peoples in the central Andes. They craft pottery, gold works, and cotton fabrics.

A.D. 400s
The Taironas build great stone cities in the Caribbean coastal region.

A.D. 600
Height of Mayan civilization

1499
Alonso de Ojeda meets Amerindians with gold ornaments.

1530
Beginning of transatlantic slave trade organized by the Portuguese in Africa.

1533
Pedro de Heredia founds Cartagena. The town becomes Colombia's main trading center and port.

1536
Jiménez de Quesada founds city of Bogotá. Belalcázar founds the city of Cali.

1558–1603
Reign of Elizabeth I of England

1620
Pilgrim Fathers sail the *Mayflower* to America.

1717
The Spanish create the Viceroyalty of New Granada to administer Colombia, Venezuela, and Ecuador.

1776
U.S. Declaration of Independence

1781
A tax rebellion becomes the first Colombian revolt against Spanish power; Napoleon Bonaparte takes over the Spanish Crown and gives it to his brother Joseph. Many Spanish colonies refuse to recognize Joseph as their ruler. Wars of independence end.

1789–1799
The French Revolution

1819
Simón Bolívar ousts the Spanish and establishes the republic of Gran Colombia.

1830
Bolívar dies. Ecuador and Venezuela gain independence. Colombia becomes the Republic of New Granada.

1914
World War I begins.

1939
World War II begins.

1948
"La Violencia" (The Violence) erupts.

1957
Women win the right to vote. The Liberal and Conservative parties form the National Front and alternate presidency for the next 16 years. The exclusion of other parties leads to outbreak of several guerrilla movements (ongoing).

1957
The Russians launch Sputnik.

1966–1969
The Chinese Cultural Revolution

IN COLOMBIA	IN THE WORLD
1974 The National Front agreement is extended for another 17 years.	
1980s Rise of the *Narcotraficantes*, or druglords	
1985 Guerrilla group M-19 occupies the Palace of Justice. Their battle with the military kills more than 100 people; Nevado del Ruiz volcano erupts.	**1986** Nuclear power disaster at Chernobyl in Ukraine
1993 The most famous druglord, Pablo Escobar, is killed.	**1991** Breakup of the Soviet Union
1999 An earthquake in Armenia, western Colombia, kills at least 1,185 people, injures more than 4,750, and leaves about 250,000 homeless; Plan Colombia is enforced in hopes of ending the Colombian armed conflict.	**1997** Hong Kong is returned to China.
2000 Pastrana's "Plan Colombia" wins $1.3 billion mainly in military aid from the United States to fight drug trafficking and rebels who profit and protect the trade.	**2001** World population surpasses 6 billion; Terrorists crash planes into New York, Washington D.C., and Pennsylvania.
2002 Independent candidate Álvaro Uribe wins a first-round presidential election.	**2004** Eleven Asia countries hit by giant tsunami, killing at least 225,000 people.
2005 Exploratory peace talks with the second biggest left-wing rebel group, the National Liberation Army (ELN), begin in Cuba.	
2006 Colombia and the United States agree on a free trade deal; by amending the constitution, President Uribe wins a second term in office.	**2008** Earthquake in Sichuan, China, kills 67,000 people.
2010 Venezuela cuts diplomatic ties with Colombia. Juan Manuel Santos takes over as president, having won easy victory in runoff election in June.	**2009** Outbreak of flu virus H1N1 around the world
2011 FARC releases several hostages, described as a unilateral "gesture of peace" to government.	**2011** Twin earthquake and tsunami disasters strike northeast Japan, leaving 14,000 dead and thousands more missing.

GLOSSARY

bogotano (bog-o-TAN-no)
Belonging to Bogotá; an inhabitant of Bogotá.

compadrazgo (kom-pah-DRAHS-go)
The spiritual relationship between a child's godparents and parents.

cartel
A group of manufacturers (in Colombia, drug traffickers) colluding to control the supply of a good so as to control prices.

cloud forest
Forest with persistent low-level cloud cover.

colegios (co-LAY-he-os)
Schools.

conquistador
A 16th-century Spanish conqueror.

cordillera
A mountain range.

creole
A person born in the West Indies or Latin America but of European, usually Spanish, ancestry.

department
What a state is called in Colombia.

El Dorado
The mythical city rumored to abound in gold.

escuelas (es-coo-AY-las)
Schools.

feria
A festival associated with a religious pilgrimage.

Happy Planet Index
A scale that measures the well-being of people in the nations of the world while taking into account their environmental impact.

llanos
Grassy lowlands.

mestizo
Someone of mixed Spanish-Indian ancestry.

mulatto
A person of mixed black and white ancestry.

picadores
A pair of horsemen in a Spanish bullfight who jab the bull with a lance.

plaza de toros (PLAH-sah de TOH-ros)
A bullfighting ring.

pre-Columbian
The pre-Columbian era incorporates all periods in Colombia's history before the appearance of significant European influences.

tejo (TAY-ho)
A traditional game resembling horseshoes.

tierra fría (tee-ERR-rah FREE-ah)
Spanish for cold land.

torero
The bullfighter who kills the bull.

torrid zone
A zone of the Earth where the sun is directly overhead.

vaquero
A Colombian cowboy.

FOR FURTHER INFORMATION

BOOKS

Croy, Anita. *National Geographic Countries of the World: Colombia.* Des Moines, IA: National Geographic Children's Books, 2008.

Gelletly, LeeAnne. *Colombia* (South America Today). Broomall, PA: Mason Crest Publishers, 2009.

Gritzner, Charles F. *Colombia* (Modern World Nations). New York: Chelsea House Publishers, 2008.

Morrison, Marion. *Colombia* (Enchantment of the World Second Series). New York: Children's Press, 2007.

Winter, Jeanette Biblioburro. *A True Story from Colombia.* La Jolla, CA : Beach Lane Books, 2010.

WEBSITES

CIA World Factbook: Colombia. www.cia.gov/library/publications/the-world-factbook/geos/co.html

Current human rights issues in Colombia. www.globalexchange.org/colombia/

General information. www.yahoo.com/Regional/Countries/Colombia/

Human rights and environmental concerns in Colombia. www.colombiasupport.net

Lonely Planet World Guide: Destination Colombia. www.lonelyplanet.com/destinations/south_america/colombia/

Various topics about the country. www.escapeartist.com/colombia1/colombia1.htm

MUSIC

Ayombe!: The Heart of Colombia's Música Vallenata. Various Artists. Smithsonian Folkways Recordings, 2008.

Colombia!: The Golden Age of Discos Fuentes. Various Artists. Soundway, 2007.

Colombia Chill: Special Blend of Colombian. Various Artists. Warner Music Latina, 2008.

VIDEO

A MI COLOMBIA. Yoyo, 2009.

Ancient Voices, Modern World: Colombia & Amazon. National Geographic, 2010.

Victor Manuel Gaviria: Medellín. Venevision International, 2007.

BIBLIOGRAPHY

BOOKS

Betancourt, Ingrid. *Even Silence Has an End: My Six Years of Captivity in the Colombian Jungle.* New York: Penguin Press HC, 2010.

Devereux, Charlie. *Colombia Handbook, 3rd: Tread Your Own Path* (Footprint—Travel Guides). Bath, UK: Footprint Handbooks, 2009.

Johnson, Jaime. *Bogotá and Beyond: A One of a Kind Guidebook to Bogotá, Colombia with over 350 Pictures.* Charleston, SC: CreateSpace, 2009.

Newton, Paula and Caputo, Lorraine. *Colombia: Viva Travel Guides.* Quito, Ecuador: Viva Publishing Network, 2010.

Porup, Jens; Raub, Kevin; Soriano, Cesar G.; and Reid, Robert. *Lonely Planet Colombia* (Country Guide). Oakland, CA: Lonely Planet, 2009.

Woods, Sarah. *Colombia* (Bradt Travel Guide). England, UK: Bradt Travel Guides, 2008.

WEBSITES

Americas Society: Colombia takes out top FARC leader. www.as-coa.org/articles/2689/Colombia_Takes_Out_Top_FARC_Leader/

Americas Society: The Andean Region at a crossroads. Economic, political and security prospects. www.as-coa.org/articles/1101/The_Andean_Region_at_a_Crossroads:_Economic,_Political,_and_Security_Prospects/

Colombia Reports.com: FARC has drug trafficking network in Brazil. http://colombiareports.com/colombia-news/news/9791-farc-have-drug-trafficking-networks-in-brazil.html.

Encyclopedia of Earth: Los Katios National Park, Colombia. www.eoearth.org/article/Los_Kat%C3%ADos_National_Park,_Colombia

INDEX

INDEX